W9-BXD-493

MEDICARE

GARLAND REFERENCE LIBRARY
OF SOCIAL SCIENCE
(Vol. 406)

MEDICARE

*A Handbook on the History and Issues of
Health Care Services for the Elderly*

William A. Pearman
and
Philip Starr

GARLAND PUBLISHING, INC. · NEW YORK & LONDON
1988

Library of Congress Cataloging-in-Publication Data

Pearman, William A., 1940–
Medicare : a handbook on the history and issues of
health care services for the elderly.

(Garland reference library of social science;
vol. 406)
Bibliography: p.
Includes indexes.
1. Medicare—Handbooks, manuals, etc.   I. Starr,
Philip, 1935– .   II. Title.   III. Series: Garland
reference library of social science; v.406.

HD7102.U4P43   1988   368.4'26'00973   88–2423
ISBN 0–8240–8391–1(alk. paper)

Printed on acid-free, 250-year-life paper
Manufactured in the United States of America

Contents

Preface

        This book serves as a basic reference for
understanding Medicare from its inception to the
mid-80s, identifies issues in the provision of
health care for the elderly, and serves as a
source for locating references and research
materials on the topic. It should prove useful
to persons working with the elderly or in the
fields related to health care services or health
care policy. It can also serve to sensitize the
lay citizen to the issues and political dynamics
that surround Medicare.

        The book consists of three sections: a
review essay, a bibliography that contains both
annotated and non-annotated listings, and an
annotated reference to The New York Times
coverage of the Medicare program.

        The review essay provides a basic description
of the Medicare program and its component parts.
Basic concepts related to Medicare are defined and
discussed. There is an analysis of events and the
political climate that preceded the enactment of
Medicare legislation and a discussion of the
program's beginnings. The issues of cost coverage
and access to the program have been consistent
concerns throughout the more than twenty years of
the program's history. They are discussed in some
detail here, both in terms of factual information
and future implications for health care services
and policy. Recent proposals to remedy and/or
expand Medicare are also discussed.

There are over one hundred annotated entries
in the bibliographic section. Sources selected for
annotation are those the authors consider to be
more important in terms of the significance of
their contribution to the overall understanding of
Medicare, or those that present an in-depth
coverage of an important Medicare-related issue.
The bibliographic references cover a time span that
ranges from the program's beginnings to 1986. In
preparing the bibliography, the authors engaged in
an extensive search of existing books, professional
journals, and other reference materials.

They solicited research papers and manuscripts from
scholars, researchers, and practitioners working in
fields related to the topic. Government documents
were also a useful source of information.

The New York Times annotations are presented
in chronological order. They are included to help
the reader develop a feel for Medicare's
development and to assist researchers and scholars
on the topic.

Medicare

REVIEW ESSAY

Medicare Description

Medicare was enacted in 1965 as Title XVIII
of the Social Security Act. It was designed to
provide health insurance to most American
citizens aged 65 and over; to certain disabled
persons under 65; and to certain workers and
their dependents for special treatment.
Medicare is federally administered and financed
for all persons eligible for Social Security
payments whether they are retired or continue to
be employed. The program has two components:
Part A, a hospital insurance program and Part B,
a supplemental medical insurance program. Both
Parts A and B require beneficiaries to pay
certain deductibles and coinsurance charges.

Part A, the hospital component of Medicare,
is funded by taxes on earnings. It covers
inpatient hospitalization, skilled nursing care,
and home care that is medically necessary. Before
Medicare will reimburse them for eligible services,
beneficiaries must pay a deductible. The amount of
the deductible has risen steadily over the years.
The initial deductible was $40. It has more than
quadrupled in the twenty years since the original
proposal. In addition, beneficiaries must pay co-
payments or have supplemental insurance for the
costs of services that exceed reimbursement
limitations. The small percentage of individuals
who are age 65 or over and not eligible for Social
Security or railroad retirement benefits may obtain

3

Part A coverage by paying a monthly premium. The
initial Medicare franchise was expanded to include
persons who are eligible for Social Security, i.e.,
chronologically, but who elect to continue to work
and have earnings. These people can apply to
participate in Part A. There is no premium cost to
them.

Part B of Medicare is a supplementary
medical insurance program for physician
services, outpatient therapy, medical equipment,
and home health care. Part B is a voluntary
program that is financed through general revenue
funds and monthly premium charges for enrollees.
As in Part A, Part B requires beneficiaries to
pay deductibles and coinsurance charges or to
carry supplemental coinsurance. Unless an
individual elects to reject enrollment in Part
B, their contribution for this program is
deducted from their monthly Social Security
check. There is also special coverage without
premium charge for a limited group of
individuals under age 65 who have severe kidney
disease.

The medical component, Part B, reimburses
the individual beneficiary directly or allows
the recipient to assign the right to claim
benefits to their physician who then bills the
insurance carrier. The percent of physicians
who accept Medicare assignment has been
decreasing steadily since the inception of the
Medicare program. It has declined from 62% at
inception to approximately 46%, currently.
Assignment is equated with 80% of the lower of a
physician's customary charge or the 75th
percentile of the prevailing charge for similar
services in the physician's geographic area,
plus a 20% contribution from the patients.
Although physicians might receive a smaller fee
by receiving payment directly from Medicare, the
payment is quicker and surer than by billing the
patient. That patients may obtain Medicare
payments on the basis of an unpaid bill is
considered a built-in weakness of the program.
Once patients receive reimbursement, they can
delay paying their provider for as long as

practically feasible. The other side of the
issue is that physicians who do not accept
assignment have a handle to force health care
costs up. Medicare is a universal insurance
program. This means that Medicare regulations
do not attend to class, race, income, or other
specific characteristics of the recipient.

From Medicare's inception, issues emerged
around the problem of coverage, either what is
covered by Medicare, or what it does not cover.
In addition, the cost of coverage both to the
recipient and to the government has been a
continuing primary issue.

Pre-Enactment and Early Development

     Although there has never been a ground
swell of support in the United States for a
national health insurance program, the American
people and their elected political
representatives have from time to time exhibited
some support for a total or partial program in
this area. The administration of Franklin Delano
Roosevelt introduced a number of ideological and
programatic reforms in the welfare and human
services area. Feeling that the time was right,
Roosevelt's successor, Harry S. Truman, proposed
a national health insurance program. The
proposal was defeated by Congress, and from that
point in the early 50's onward, the focus
shifted from a general health plan to a specific
one. Health insurance for the elderly seemed to
be a more politically acceptable idea than a
universal program.

     The term "Medicare" was the label attached
to a state-sponsored-means health program
proposed by Health, Education, and Welfare
Secretary, Arthur Fleming, during the Eisenhower
administration. Although the eventual Medicare
plan introduced in the Lyndon Johnson era was
radically different, the term "Medicare" stuck.
Richard Nixon, Eisenhower's Vice President,
advocated a means-tested insurance program for
the elderly in his 1960 campaign for the
Presidency. The Democratic candidate, John F.
Kennedy, criticized Nixon and promised that if
elected, he would propose health insurance that

6

would protect the elderly regardless of their finances. Health insurance in these debates was synonymous with hospital insurance. The proposal advocated by Kennedy was known as the King-Anderson Bill, named after its congressional sponsors.

From the very beginning, the Medicare program was thought of as an insurance program, not a welfare program. The debate of the early 60s focused almost exclusively on assistance with insurance premiums; the organization of health services or the method of determining fee structures received little attention. This emphasis on the insurance premiums may have been the only way that Medicare could have been enacted into law. Although this tactic helped adopt the program, it kept attention away from the matters that would become persistent controversial issues over time, the possible increases in costs of health services from physicians and hospitals. Over the course of the debate, assistance with hospital costs was the big issue. The more comprehensive plan that was eventually adopted emerged only near the end of the drive for adoption of Medicare in 1965. In the final rush, the Republican means-tested program took a form that became the current Medicaid program. Medicaid is a state administered program for the financially needy. It varies by state in terms of scope and implementation details. The program has been plagued by problems of inconsistency that might have been avoided if more time had been taken to consider initial rationale and program details.

A number of factors are generally cited to explain how the Medicare program was able to pass Congress in 1965. Among these was a steady increase in the number of Americans age 50 and over. This number increased significantly in the late 1950s and early 1960s, the years immediately preceding passage of Medicare. The increased politicization of the elderly and the development of their self-interest and advocacy groups, especially the National Council of Senior Citizens was another factor in pressure to adopt Medicare.

These pressures were aided by an increase in the
number of liberals and/or Democrats elected to the
89th Congress in the Johnson landslide
Presidential victory of 1964.

In January 1965, as part of his State of the
Union message, Lyndon Johnson urged Congress to
pass the Medicare Bill. He announced that
Medicare was his top priority and that he planned
to finance it through the Social Security Trust
Fund. The American Medical Association responded
with a counterplan that utilized Blue Cross/Blue
Shield as a private insurance carrier and was
addressed to the health of financially needy
elderly only. In his budget message that he
delivered later in January, President Johnson
proposed substantial increases in Social Security
taxes to pay for the Medicare program. Johnson
appealed for public support for the program. He
received an endorsement by organized labor through
the AFL-CIO. The American Medical Association
continued its opposition and was joined by the
American Dental Association. The American Health
Insurance Association charged that Medicare would
drive private insurance companies out of business.

An important figure in the battle for
Medicare was Congressman Wilbur Mills. Mills was
Chairman of the Congressional Ways and Means
Committee. This committee was responsible for the
introduction of all tax-related legislation.
Mills, who initially opposed the Bill, lent his
support and was the architect of a congressional
expansion of the Bill. This expansion co-opted
diverse interests and integrated their concerns
with Johnson's plan. Issues of who was covered,
what was covered, and how it was to be financed
emerged. The expanded plan was quite comprehensive.
It went far beyond hospitalization. As various
concerns were addressed by an expanded bill,
opposition began to fade. The opposition that
remained centered more on the financial integrity
of the Social Security System than on Medicare itself.

On April 9, 1965, the House of Representatives
approved the Medicare Bill. The old King-Anderson Bill
from the Kennedy era provided substance for the hospital
insurance aspect, Part A. Republican Congressman John
Byrnes instigated a medical/providers proposal that
became Part B. The means test aspect that the American
Medical Association used to limit the scope of Medicare
gave rise to Medicaid as a state-operated income-based
supplemental plan. All interests seemed to be
represented in some way. Special interests including
hospitals, physicians, the health insurance industry and
the drug industry were all accommodated. When passage
of Medicare appeared inevitable, the American Medical
Association spent its energies in steering the debate
away from issues that involved the pricing of health
services. It charged that Medicare would lead to a
decline in the quality of health care. Following
passage of Medicare by the House of Representatives, but
prior to final Senate action, the American Medical
Association made a final ideological appeal through a
public advertising campaign. They charged that Medicare
would lead to federalized hospitals and socialized
medicine. It was depicted as a threat to private
enterprise, possibly un-American in ideology. Some
individual physicians threatened a boycott of the
program.

The general public seemed ready to accept the
Medicare proposal. Public opinion polls reported that
about two-thirds of the population favored some assistance in the financing of personal health services. No
less than 63% approved the program before the 89th
Congress. The fact that the American Association of
Retired Persons was not in the forefront of support for
Medicare may seem strange. This organization assumed a
position similar to that proposed by the American
Medical Association. They backed an administrative
coalition composed of trustees from the health care
industry, private business, and aged interest groups.
The American Association of Retired Persons has been
concerned with protecting the income of senior citizens.
Perhaps they perceived the linkage of Medicare to the
Social Security System as a threat to their best long-
term economic interests.

Finally on July 10, 1965, the Senate approved the
Medicare Bill. Last ditch opposition came from Senator

Russell Long, who pointed out that the bill did not deal
with catastrophic illness. Long sought to shift the
focus of the bill from limited benefits for all aged to
unrestricted benefits for the poor. However, President
Johnson prevailed with the Senate Finance Committee and
the House of Representatives and the Senate worked to
iron out their differences. The final text called for
expansion of the Social Security System to provide
hospitalization, nursing home care, home nursing
services, and outpatient diagnostic services to all
Americans over 65 years of age. The Bill also included
a proposal for supplementary federal insurance to cover
physician bills at a premium cost of $3 per month. In a
salute to Harry Truman's earlier efforts for a Medicare-
like program, President Johnson signed the Medicare Bill
into law in Independence, Missouri, on July 31, 1965.
The law was to take effect on July 1, 1966.

Organized medical opposition to Medicare continued
even after the passage of the law. Members of the
Association of American Physicians and Surgeons urged
its members to boycott implementation of Medicare. The
American Medical Association took the position that
individual physicians could boycott Medicare but that
the boycotters were acting in their own interest and not
in concert with the Association. After a final dispute
between hospital representatives and third-party
intermediary interest groups over reimbursement
procedures, the President of the American Medical
Association, in a less-than-enthusiastic appeal in
November of 1965, urged all doctors to cooperate with
Medicare. The AMA cooperation was motivated by a desire
to have the negative aspects of the Medicare Bill
reflect on the government and not on the medical
community. From that point on, AMA and federal
government representatives worked behind the scenes to
achieve compromises on their differences over Medicare.

The 1960s were a time of great racial tension in
the United States. The implementation of the Medicare
legislation became entangled in the civil rights
struggle. The issue was the non-compliance of
hospitals, particularly in the South, with the 1964
Civil Rights Act. This act barred discrimination by any
institution that receives federal financial aid. The
Department of Health, Education, and Welfare monitored

progress in compliance, and hospitals, fearing a loss
of funds, quickly responded to this problem. By July 1,
1966, HEW reported that 92% of hospitals were in
compliance with the Civil Rights Act and ready to
participate in Medicare.

The requirement of taking loyalty oaths when
receiving certain governmental funds or benefits was
another issue in Medicare implementation. The original
Medicare legislation carried a provision for a loyalty
oath by recipients of Medicare benefits. In January of
1967, the U.S. Department of Justice decided against
enforcing this provision. The Supreme Court later ruled
that the oath was unconstitutional.

Cost was an issue with Medicare from the very
beginning. Within six weeks following the beginning of
the Medicare program, President Johnson ordered an
inquiry into rising medical costs. An indication of the
dramatic rise in health care costs is derived from The
New York Times reports of that period. On August 19,
1966, the paper reported that some New York doctors had
raised fees for the treatment of the aged as much as
300%. In September, the paper reported that during the
decade of the 1960s hospital bills were increasing at a
rate five times that of the cost of living.

As rates of hospital utilization and the rising
costs thereof that were associated with the Medicare
program became known after the first year or two of
operation, Congress amended the initial Medicare
benefits in an attempt to keep the program in a sound
fiscal state.

The program paid out $3.2 billion in its first
year. A question that soon emerged was whether a
standardized uniform reimbursement fee structure
for Medicare should be set in order to combat
escalated physician and hospital fees. The AMA
opposed such standardization, but governmental and
senior citizens groups advocated it. The AMA
charged that the basis of escalating costs was
governmental administrative in nature and not
related to medical or hospital fees.

Increasingly, cost containment became the
focus of Congressional debate and of exchanges
between government and health care representatives.
From the time of passage of Medicare legislation to
the end of the first two years of implementation,
i.e., the three year period 1965-1968, medical care
costs doubled. For the year 1968, the American
Hospital Association projected the increase in
hospital costs to be 12.4%. In September 1970 an
AMA study of the federal budget indicated that
annual government expenditures for medicine and
health tripled in the previous five years.

There were several early attempts to extend
the Medicare franchise. In November, 1967,
President Johnson sought to cover 1.5 million
disabled workers under age 65. The move was
rejected by a U.S. Senate Committee that dealt with
Social Security and Medicare cost issues. In
December, 1967, Medicare was extended to cover
citizens of the District of Columbia. The monthly
premium of $3.00 for the voluntary insurance part
of Medicare was increased to $4.00 at that time.

As the decade of the 70s began, the provisions
of Public Law 92-603 expanded the Medicare net
beyond the elderly to include certain disabled
persons and those in need of kidney transplants and
renal dialysis. Elderly previously excluded from
Medicare coverage were also brought into the
program, but at a substantial personal premium. A
60-day lifetime reserve was added to existing
hospital coverage. Liberalization of Part B added
physical therapy and speech pathology benefits.
There was some tightening of the program as well.
For example, a stricter interpretation was enforced
of the phrase "medically necessary" in relation to
nursing home care.

Despite rising costs, Medicare still did not
adequately address the health needs of the elderly.
In January 1971, a Senate Committee on Aging
stated that Medicare was paying less than one-half
of the health bill for persons 65 years of age and
older. The issues in the Medicare debates did not
focus on eligibility or services but rather
physician and hospital payment and costs. The

Nixon Administration continuously proposed benefit
and payment cuts and sought ways of passing health
costs on to the private sector rather than the
public sector. Patients' hospital costs were
increased to offset governmental costs.

Economic Issues

The 1972 Presidential campaign between Richard
Nixon and George McGovern and the pursuit of the
Democratic nomination prior to the campaign
witnessed calls for expansion of Medicare to
various categories of persons and services not
previously covered. The campaign also saw a
reemergence of calls for National Health Insurance
by various political leaders. The AMA and the
Academy of Family Physicians rebuffed these calls.
They pointed to potential cost abuses and advocated
a "medicredit," a tax credit for the purchase of
private health insurance. As the skyrocketing
costs of hospital care became known and a more
conservative political constituency came into
power, the pressures for Medicare expansion and
interest in National Health Insurance subsided.
Cost containment in the health care sector became a
major policy focus.

The attack on Medicare costs swept across
various fronts. In general, cost strategies
resulted in reduced services or benefits or raised
the consumer's responsibilities through increased
coinsurance and deductible payments. Less obvious
tactics were also attempted. For example, the
vague language of the Medicare legislation allowed
private interests a great deal of flexibility in
pricing. Take for example the term "customary or
prevailing charge." How should physicians be
grouped in terms of geographic area and practice
specialty to determine customary or prevailing
charges? The government has delegated the

14

responsibility for this dilemma to Blue Shield.
However, pricing was not being determined in a
uniform way. Insurance carriers often paid more to
doctors for treating Medicare recipients than they
did for providing for those enrolled in their
private plans. Attention turned to examination of
the administration of payment both in terms of
payment mechanisms and regulations.

In 1972, Congress introduced an economic index
into the Medicare payment formula. This allowed
the prevailing charge for a service to rise only as
much as inflation in general. The United States
General Accounting Office found that under this
guideline, Medicare costs, i.e., prevailing
charges, rose 3.6% in the period 1973-1978. They
also found that private pay charges exceeded
Medicare charges 40% of the time.

A special study committee, the Perkins
Committee, was formed to study the administration
of Medicare contracts by insurance carriers. In
February 1973, the Committee recommended that HEW
develop better ways of measuring carrier
performance, ways of rewarding good and terminating
poor insurance carriers, and ways of improving cost
reporting and accounting. One issue was that since
specialists were paid more than generalists for
their services, how did insurance companies arrive
at their determination of who was a specialist, and
what could they do to stem the wish of generalists
who sought to be labeled as specialists. The
Health Care Financing Commission struggled with
these cost implication issues and devised stop-gap
solutions.

Refusal by physicians to accept Medicare
assignment fueled the cost problem for consumers.
As the difference between Medicare's reasonable
charges and the physician's actual charges grew,
the number of doctors refusing to accept assignment
increased. In 1969, approximately 62% of all
physicians accepted assignment. By the end of the
70s, the rate was just over 50%, and as we move
through the 80s, the percentage is down to 45%.

The rate varies by region of the country. The
highest rate of acceptance of assignment is found
in New England, while the lowest rate is in the
Pacific Northwest region. Faced with the downturn
of physician willingness to accept Medicare
assignment, consumers signed up for Medigap, third
party, or coinsurance programs in record numbers.
As a result there developed the problem of
fraudulent insurance companies and schemes to milk
the elderly of insurance dollars. The decline in
assignment acceptance in effect denies the reality
of universal coverage. It is contradictory to the
rationale behind Medicare.

From the National Health Planning and
Resources Act of 1974 on into the 1980s, hospitals
lobbied Congress to prevent the introduction of
uniform reporting and accounting regulations for
Medicare reimbursement. Hospitals argued that to
implement such systems would cost dollars and raise
costs. They sought to preserve their freedom to
price services as they wished. Alternatives to fee
for service received an occasional impetus from
Congress. There were attempts by the Social
Security Administration to enroll recipients in
pre-paid health maintenance organizations during
the Nixon and the Ford administrations. These
attempts met with little success.

The problem of vagueness in Medicare language
was referred to above. Another language problem
that contributes to increased Medicare costs is the
lack of uniform language in describing treatment or
diagnosis. Physicians found that creative or
embellished language could enhance the amount of
their reimbursement. It is no wonder that the
Health Care Financing Administration came to feel
the need for a standardized medical procedure and
terminology coding system.

In its original version, Title XVIII
contained provisions for utilization review
procedures that addressed service errors, but
again, the vagaries of how to define such errors,
how to detect them, and how to correct them soon
proved utilization review ineffective. The

original utilization review process and procedures
gave rise in 1972 to the initiation of review
organizations called Professional Standard Review
Mechanisms, PSROs. From the start the PSROs were
citicized as soft, inaccurate, and weak in terms of
teeth to check providers. The Carter
Administration of 1976-1980 kept pressure on the
PSROs to prove their worth through tough reviews.

In addition to attempts to enforce some type
of review processes before treatment would be
authorized, and as checks on the efficacy of health
care delivery systems, there was also an effort to
avoid construction of unnecessary facilities. The
effort to control new construction came through the
requirements of the certificate of needs program.
Through this program, hospitals had to show that a
need for expansion existed before new construction
could begin. Despite these strategies of cost
containment, there was not strong evidence that
costs were being effectively contained. In its
initial months, the Reagan administration seemed
displeased with these strategies. Instead, there
was interest in promoting competition between
hospitals as a means of cost control.

The trend of rising coinsurance requirements
and increasing out-of-pocket expenses continued
into the 80s. This has severe implications for
persons who are financially dependent on the Social
Security System as their sole or main source of
income and for victims of catastrophic illness.
Implications are even greater for those persons who
are both poor and suffering from severe illness.

We can gain some insight into the dimension of
the problem by considering that about one-third of
all expenditures on health care are for the needs
of those 65 years of age and over, and that the
aged are paying roughly one-third of the total cost
of their own health bills. The spiral of costs is
underlined by the fact that throughout the 70s,
health costs outdistanced the Consumer Price Index
to the extent that in 1970 health care accounted
for 7.2% of the Gross National Product, but by 1981
it had grown to 9.8%.

As an illustration of how the elderly
themselves are affected by rising health costs,
consider that from 1966-1981, the premium for Part
A was increased four and one-half times, the
premium for Part B was increased by almost three
and one-half times. Part B copayments were held
constant at 20% of costs, but since costs rose
dramatically, the copayment also spiraled.
Costs of hospital stays beyond a 90-day period
increased in ratio to the Part A premium, i.e.,
from $20 to $90 per diem. The Part B deductible
rose from $50 to $70 to $75. The elderly spend
one-fifth of their income on medical care and as
cost shifts to beneficiaries continue, this figure
is expected to rise also.

The Reagan administration and Congress
addressed a series of Social Security/Medicare
financing problems in 1981. They were concerned
about the long-term financial outlook. The result
was HR 4331, which authorized the Old Age Survivors
Insurance, the Disability Insurance Program, and
the Medicare Trust Funds to borrow among themselves
for a one-year period. The intent was to delay
cash flow problems until a more permanent financing
solution could be found. In January 1983 the
Social Security Reform Commission proposed a
long term phase-in program to relieve Social
Security and Disability pressures.

Now, in the late 80s, Medicare appears to be
financially healthy, but problems are projected for
the Medicare Trust Fund after 1990. One of the
reasons for the expected problems is the increase
in the number of aged, plus increased life
expectancies. If the 10-20% per annum increases in
hospital costs evidenced in the early 80s continue,
these problems could be severe.

Some important new directions in Medicare
financing emerged from the Tax Equity and Fiscal
Responsibility Act of 1981. These changes are
incorporated in Public Law 97-248. Beneficiaries
were affected as follows: 1) annual automatic
increases in the Part B deductible were initiated,
2) the Part B premium was set at a constant
percentage of costs, 3) employers are required to

offer the same health benefits to workers ages
65-69 and their dependents as to younger workers.
The law downgraded Medicare from the first to
second payer of health costs and shifted more
responsibility to the private insurance sector.

In addition to increased costs for
beneficiaries, the Tax Equity and Fiscal
Responsibility Act also led to consumer gains. The
main gain was the addition of benefits to provide
additional low-cost care for the terminally ill.
It included services such as medical social
services; counselling; nursing and physician
services; home health aid; therapies and medical
supplies; and short-term hospital care. Hospice
care and drugs were also provided for at a 5%
copayment.

The pool of Medicare revenues was increased in
that federal employees were now required to buy
into the Medicare program for hospital insurance.
Although this provided a temporary shot of funding,
long-term effects will only be known as claims from
these federal employees are measured against their
payments.

Public Law 97-248 affected providers as well
as beneficiaries. It contained direct attempts to
control reimbursement. Among these attempts were:
1) setting hospital budget targets for
expenditures, 2) denying duplicate payment for
outpatient services, 3) eliminating private room
subsidies, 4) refusing reimbursement for
ineffective medicines. Limits on Medicare payment
for ancillary costs were also set. A cap of 9.7%
was placed on overall hospital rate increases per
discharge, and incentives to stay under that were
added.

Public Law 97-248 and the subsequent Social
Security Amendments of 1983 (P.L. 98-21) introduced
one of the most controversial changes in Medicare,
the classification and reimbursement scheme known
as diagnostic related groups (DRGs). Beginning
with a phase-in in October 1983, hospitals are paid
a specific reimbursement on the basis of a
previously established flat fee per illness

classification. Previously, hospitals were
reimbursed after services were rendered. They were
paid for the total cost of each hospital day of
care as well as for ancillary services. That
system encouraged full use of hospital beds and
services; essentially, it guaranteed payment for
all services. Paying hospitals an amount fixed in
advance is viewed as a move to contain costs and
encourage more efficient manpower and service
utilization.

The DRGs have come under a barrage of
criticism. It is felt that the system does not
allow for individual differences in terms of
overall health state, or for differences in severity
of illness. Many are concerned that the DRGs could
lead to premature discharge that contributes to a
deterioration in patient health. Critics charge
that patients are being discharged "quicker and
sicker." The quality of service, particularly
nursing services, are also being questioned. At
this time, it is too premature to measure the
effectiveness of DRGs for cost saving and to balance
this against quality of health care.

We must ask whether hospitals and physicians
will absorb the effects of the changes that stem
from Public Law 97-248, or will the payments
previously made by Medicare now be shifted to
Medicare beneficiaries, private pay patients, and
third-party insurers. Will providers react by
refusing assignment from Medicare, increasing their
charges, and forcing Medicare beneficiaries to pay a
greater share of medical costs directly to them?

Although President Reagan proposed more funds
for Medicare in 1984 than he did in 1983, he also
sought budget cutting beyond the amount that would
otherwise be required to maintain existing Medicare
program benefits. Three factors combine to paint a
bleak picture for Medicare financing for the
remainder of the 80s. These are the increased life
expectancy and increased numbers of aged, the
federal budget deficit, and the fact that although
inflation in general waned in 1984 and 1985,
Medicare expenditures continued to grow faster than
the rate of inflation. The options for cost

containment appear to fall in one of two directions:
1) reduce the reimbursement rates directly affecting
the providers or 2) reduce benefits and increase coinsurance and affect beneficiaries. Reagan
administration announcements of July, 1985 indicate
that both routes will be followed in a modest rather
than severe fashion.

If the Medicare system of the future is to
achieve cost containment, it will need to create
disincentives rather than incentives for increasing
health care profits in the private sector. It will
also need to address ways of providing for chronic
illness, disability, and rehabilitative care as
opposed to a current emphasis on acute care.
Beneficiaries need to be more enlightened as to the
costs of treatment and the availability and
consequences of alternative treatment. Consumers
could bear more responsibility for their health care
and possibly contribute to cost savings, but they
need more information than they presently have.

Access and Other Issues

From the description of the Medicare program
offered earlier, we have little difficulty in
viewing Medicare as a bona fide insurance program.
The symbolism of insurance and universal coverage of
people from all classes helped Medicare avoid the
stigma of a welfare or give away program.

A legitimate question concerns whether the
health of the aged has improved as a result of
Medicare. Those who answer in the affirmative argue
that since the inception of Medicare, the number of
persons in what is called the old-old or frail
elderly category, i.e. 75 years of age or more, has
increased. They cite that people are living longer
and attribute this to an increased availability of
health care and access to it via Medicare. They
also note that the number of acute conditions for
those 65 years of age and over has declined since
1965 and the percentage of aged with some degree of
limitation due to chronic conditions has declined.
These statements might all be factual, but it would
be a mistake to conclude that Medicare is a primary
cause of the changes cited. Some evidence exists to
suggest that the number of days of restricted
activity for the elderly has decreased since the
advent of Medicare and that Medicare might be linked
to lower mortality rates for specific diseases.
What is probably an accurate statement is that the
disabled and persons with chronic kidney disease
decreased their disability and physical discomfort
levels as a result of Medicare. A safe conclusion
is that the program has made some difference in the
overall health of its beneficiaries.

Some would argue that physician contact or utilization has remained constant for the elderly. This is true, but the rate has changed vis-a-vis achieved characteristics of the aged. Physician contact has increased for the aged poor, but decreased for the nonpoor aged.

One of the most staggering changes in health care statistics since Medicare's inception is a rise in surgical rates. During the first 10 years of the program the number of surgeries for persons 65 years of age and older increased approximately 2 1/2 times, from 6,000 for every 100,000 persons to 15,000 plus for every 100,000 persons. Whether this results in an improvement in health care remains to be answered.

Medicare did little to ameliorate geographic barriers to medical care. The program contributed to maintaining differences in physician fees between metropolitan and non-metropolitan areas. Medicare did little to encourage physicians to locate or relocate in medically underserved areas.

Medicare is described as a program of universal coverage; it is based on age not financial need. This universal coverage means that high-income elderly could reap substantial subsidies from the program, but it also means that differences in hospital care based on race, and socio-economic status factors could be narrowed.

Since Medicare is not based on need, there is a concern as to whether Medicare meets the needs of those in poorer circumstances. A need entitlement program as opposed to a universal program would direct scarce resources to those with greatest financial need. A universal needs based program open to all ages might soften the resentment that some people have toward the elderly. As benefits for the elderly increase, and as the elderly become an increasingly larger segment of the population, we can expect increased estrangement between the young and old in our society. A universal needs program would lessen resentment from younger groups about benefits for the nonpoor elderly.

One access related issue surrounding Medicare
has been how to insure that health care access is
geographically distributed or how to prevent the
growth of medical ghettos. The program has probably
done more to be sure that services are available,
than it has to insure the quality of the services.
For example, the initial Medicare statute required
that certification of hospitals for Medicare
participation depend on certification from the Joint
Commission on Accreditation of Hospitals.
Initially, only 60% of hospitals met this
requirement; most were urban as opposed to rural in
location. It was decided to allow nonaccredited
hospitals to apply to Medicare for certification.
The result was that only about 8% of the
nonaccredited hospitals that applied were rejected.

As stated earlier, Medicare does not cover long-
term nursing home care. This is possible only
through Medicaid which is tied to income. Due to
the increase in the number of very old or frail
elderly and the increase in the number of elderly
who live alone, this raises questions about the
adequacy of Medicare coverage. Adequacy questions
can be raised about the range of health services,
why are some covered and others not covered. The
avoidance of long term nursing home care and
liberalization of home health benefits alternatives
to institutionalization are perceived by many as
cost effective.

An underlying problem is that different people
have different needs; what is provided through
Medicare may not meet specific needs of a given
elderly or disabled individual. An individual's
needs may be in an excluded category such as home-
care, day-care, respite-care, foster-care,
protective-care, or as often the case with our
elderly population, dental-care or mental health
care. It appears that what is really needed is a
range or cafeteria approach to options rather than
an all purpose solution.

A continuum of services might be offered from
which individuals pick and choose according to their
needs. There could be a dollar ceiling on benefit
costs or some other method to equalize benefits.

This could help answer the problem of adequate for
whom - each according to need, either medical or
medical and financial.

The intent behind Medicare was to protect the
income of the elderly. This is why Medicare was
linked to social security. This may have worked for
some, but not all. We need to examine placing caps
on cost sharing by individuals. Perhaps need
coverage can be addressed by linking income to co-
payment costs.

Medicare has become a standard for indicating
government's role in health care. It has fed into a
general rise in the proportion of all personal
medical expenditures paid for by the government.
That proportion has more than doubled since 1965.
The role of government in health care has been
legitimated; it is no longer a question. However,
because of the attention given to the costs of
Medicare, interest in National Health Insurance
has probably lessened also.

Recent Issues

The current issues facing Medicare are the result of its objective being attained, i.e., improving access to health care. As a result of this success, life expectancy has significantly increased with the greatest percentage increase belonging to the frail elderly cohort (75 years of age or older). Because of its successes, the costs of operating Medicare have become "astronomical." These costs are due to the mere number of elderly living and the escalating cost of keeping them alive.

Currently, efforts to curtail costs have focused on increasing the deductible and co-payments as well as freezing physician fees. Unfortunately, this approach has resulted in the elderly paying a greater share of their health care cost than they did prior to the enactment of Medicare. The continuation of this approach will result in reduced access of the elderly to health care. The present approach does nothing about meeting the long-term health care needs of the frail elderly.

The alternatives to the current approach are: 1) the enactment of National Health Insurance or at least a catastrophic insurance program and 2) application of the British cost containment model to the American scene. In regard to the former, National Health Insurance was not enacted out of recognition of its exorbitant costs. Catastrophic insurance has to be enacted because Medicare is not designed to meet the long-term care needs of the frail elderly. If not enacted, not only will

26

Medicare financially fail but the needs of the elderly will not be met.

The British model should be rejected. It is rooted in the premise that people over 65 should be denied costly medical procedures such as organ transplants or renal dialysis. This approach runs counter to our humanitarian value orientation.

In his State of the Union message in 1986, Ronald Reagan called catastrophic health insurance a top national priority. He charged Health and Human Services Secretary Otis R. Bowen to develop a plan to meet the catastrophic health care needs of Americans of all ages. By not limiting the plan to older Americans, Reagan might have defused some of the negativism against Medicare and increased benefits for the elderly.

Congressman Claude Pepper, Chairman of the Sub-committee on Health and Long-term Care of the Select Committee on Aging of the House of Representatives charged that no long-term health care system is complete without a home health care component. He described it as a humanitarian alternative to institutionalization and cautioned against continued scaling back of home care through subtle and unsubtle means. The Reagan administration had begun to cut back on amount and kinds of reimbursement to home care providers. Pepper was joined in his crusade by Senators Frank E. Moss and John Heinz. Heinz contended that the Reagan administration was being "penny wise and pound foolish," that failure to provide home care could lead to increased hospitalization and increased nursing home costs.

The home care controversy stemmed in part from the Medicare Hospice Benefit enacted in 1982. This benefit provided for home care for the terminally ill. Home health costs then increased and by 1986 it had become the fastest growing part of the Medicare program. By targeting home care providers for cost reductions, the Reagan administration sought to keep expenditures at then current levels. This in effect reduced benefits.

28 MEDICARE

In December 1986, Otis Bowen presented a wide
range of programs to protect Americans against the
costs of catastrophic illness. Catastrophic illness
was defined as either a short-term condition
requiring intensive acute services or a lingering
illness requiring many years of care. Bowen's
proposal mainly addressed linkage of Medicare to
catastrophic illness coverage. He proposed
expanding Medicare so that no beneficiary would have
to pay more than $2,000 a year for acute care. The
cost of the additional coverage would be an
additional $4.92 per month in Medicare premiums. Of
the 28 million elderly people covered by Medicare at
the time of Bowen's proposal, it was estimated that
800,000 annually faced out-of-pocket costs that
exceeded $2,000 for acute care. Part of Bowen's
proposal called for tax incentives that would
encourage individuals to save money and private
companies to provide coverage for long-term care in
nursing homes.

In February 1987, President Reagan offered what
he termed a "giant step" toward catastrophic health
insurance. Picking up on Bowen's proposal, Reagan
called for Medicare coverage for over-65 acute
illness, a limitation on out-of-pocket health
expenses to $2,000 a year, and an increased Medicare
Part B premium. Reagan, however, did not address
long-term nursing home care, nor other major health
expense items of the elderly such as prescriptions
or care for Alzheimer's Disease. Representative
Pepper, Senator Heinz, and Senator Ted Kennedy saw
Reagan's proposals as a minimum or a beginning.
Conservative politicians favored greater reliance on
private insurance and less governmental
intervention.

The future of Medicare remains clouded. New
issues will emerge as the program struggles to
survive and to maintain an insurance-type image, and
as consumers, political action, and older American
lobbyist groups make new and increased demands.

1. Abdellah, Faye G. "Long Term Care Policy Issues:
    Alternatives to Institutional Care." THE ANNALS
    OF THE AMERICAN ACADEMY OF POLITICAL & SOCIAL
    SCIENCE, 438 (July 1978): 28-39.

    A demographic and descriptive picture is given of
    the elderly's health care concerns in the U.S.
    Affordable yet quality care provision is addressed.
    The appropriateness of institutionalization of the
    elderly is examined, and noninstitutional alternatives
    are offered.

2. Aday, LuAnn. "The Impact of Health Policy on Access to
    Medical Care."   THE MILBANK MEMORIAL FUND QUARTERLY,
    54 (Spring 1976): 215-223.

    Data from nationwide surveys of health-services
    utilization and expenditures, conducted in 1963
    and 1970, are used to compute a social-indicator type
    measure of access to medical care. These data confirm
    that the poor gained better access to health care,
    relative to the nonpoor, between 1963, when Medicare
    and Medicaid did not exist, and 1970, when they did.
    High-income persons with a regular family doctor, and
    middle- and low-income persons with no regular source
    of health care, had considerably lower access to
    medical care in 1970. Many poor with no regular
    health care provider continued to experience
    barriers to entry.

3. Aday, LuAnn, and Andersen, R. ACCESS TO MEDICAL CARE.
    Ann Arbor, MI: Health Administration Press, 1975.

4. Albrecht, Gary L. "Cost Containment as a Social Control
    Strategy: The Case of Health Care." Paper, Society
    for the Study of Social Problems, New York, N.Y.:
    Aug. 1980.

5. Alford, Robert. HEALTH CARE POLITICS. Chicago, ILL:
    University of Chicago Press, 1976.

6. American Association of Retired Persons. "Misinter-
    pretation of DRG Rules Causes Concern." AARP NEWS
    BULLETIN, 26 (May 1985): 1.

7. Anderson, Gerald, and Ginsburg, Paul B. "Medicare Pay-
    ment and Hospital Capital: Future Policy Options."
    HEALTH AFFAIRS (Fall 1984): 35-48.

8. Anderson, Gerald, and Knickman, James. "Adverse
   Selection Under a Voucher System: Grouping
   Medicare Recipients by Level of Expenditure."
   INQUIRY, 21 (Summer 1984): 135-143.

9. Armour, P.K., Estes, C.C., and Noble, M.L.
   "Implementing the Older Americans Act." in R.B.
   Hudson (Ed.), THE AGING IN POLITICS: PROCESS AND
   POLICY. Springfield, ILL: Charles C. Thomas,
   1981.

10. Arnett, Ross H. III, et al. "Health Spending
    Trends in the 1980's; Adjusting to Financial
    Incentives." HEALTH CARE FINANCING REVIEW, 6
    (Spring 1985): 1-25.

11. Arnett, Ross H. III, et al. "Projections of Health
    Care Spending to 1990." HEALTH CARE FINANCING
    REVIEW, 7 (Spring 1986): 1-86.

12. Atkins, G. Lawrence. "The Economic Status of the
    Oldest Old." MILBANK MEMORIAL FUND QUARTERLY,
    63 (1985): 395-419.

13. Azzarto, Jacqueline. "Medicalization of the
    Problems of the Elderly." HEALTH AND SOCIAL
    WORK, 11 (Summer 1986): 189-195.

14. Ball, Robert M. "Insuring Our Future: The
    Financing of Social Security and Medicare."
    NATIONAL VOTER, 36 (March/April 1986): 6-15.

15. Ball, Robert M. "Medicare: Expectations, Accom-
    plishments and Next Steps." GENERATIONS, 4
    (May 1980): 36-37.

16. Ball, Robert M. SOCIAL SECURITY: TODAY AND TOMOR-
    ROW. New York: Columbia University Press, 1978.

17. Ball, Robert M. "National Health Insurance:
    Comments on Selected Issues." SCIENCE, 200
    (May 26, 1978): 864-870.

Medicare has functioned as a national health
insurance system for twelve years, and its
administration involves all functions, institutions, and personnel which an extended plan would
involve. This article suggests it might be more
desirable to adopt an approach making the government the active purchaser of health care, with its
own guidelines on what medical services are
desired.

18. Belgrave, Linda Liska; Lavin, Bebe; Breslau,
     Naomi; and Haug, Marie R. "Stereotyping of the
     Aged by Medical Students." GERONTOLOGY AND
     GERIATRICS EDUCATION, 3 (Fall 1981): 37-44.

Students at two medical schools were surveyed
as to attitudes toward the aged. Control
variables did not explain students stereotypes.
Students entering family practice or internal
medicine showed less stereotyping than those
planning careers in surgery. Because of a
perceived association between meeting health
needs of the elderly and the attitude of physicians, the authors suggest a need for increased
training in gerontology in medical schools.

19. Bendel, Jean Pierre. "Hospitalization of Elderly
     in a General Hospital: Patient Characteristics,
     Department of Hospitalization and Length of
     Stay." Paper, World Congress of The Inter-
     national Sociological Association: Aug. 1982.

The paper discusses the effects of sex, marital
status, type of admission, and discharge status on
hospital usage of several age groups of elderly.
Significant differences are found between the age
groups with respect to the department of hospitalization and length of stay.

20. Berk, Marc L., and Widensky, Gail R. "Health Care
     of the Poor Elderly: Supplementing Medicare."
     THE GERONTOLOGIST, 25 (June 1985): 311-315.

21. Berliner, Howard. "Origins of Health Insurance
     for the Aged." INTERNATIONAL JOURNAL OF HEALTH
     SERVICES, 1973: 465-473.

22.   Binstock, Robert H., and Shanas, Ethel, eds.
      HANDBOOK OF AGING AND THE SOCIAL SCIENCES,
      2nd Ed. New York: Van Nostrand, Reinhold
      Co., 1985.

23.   Birnbaum, H.; Swearingen, C., and Dunlop, B.
      "Implementing Community-Based Long Term Care:
      Experience of New York's Long-Term Home Health
      Care Program." THE GERONTOLOGIST, 24, (August
      1984): 380-386.

24.   Bishop, Barbara, and Bodenheimer, Thomas. "The
      Futility of Reformism: Community-Worker Control
      and the 'Dellums Bill'." SYNTHESIS, 1 (Winter
      1976): 62-72.

      A discussion of the failure of health care
      reform in the U.S., this article points to those
      who have benefitted the most from Medicare and
      Medicaid legislation as: drug, insurance, and
      medical supply corporations. The "Dellums Bill"
      proposed a system of neighborhood health centers,
      designed to benefit the working class. By
      structuring the bill according to traditional
      bourgeois democratic procedures, vested interests
      insured that this and not the working class would
      ultimately control the "neighborhood" based
      system.

25.   Blake, J. Herman. "'Doctor Can't Do Me No Good':
      Social Concomitants of Health Care Attitudes and
      Practices among Elderly Blacks in Isolated Rural
      Populations." THE BLACK SOCIOLOGIST, 8 (Fall
      1978): 1-13.

      Observation and interviews with elderly blacks
      of Sea Islands of South Carolina and Georgia show
      a generally negative attitude toward medical prac-
      titioners and a disinclination to follow
      prescribed treatment regimens.

26.   Blum, Stephen R., and Minkler, Meredith. "Toward
      a Continuum of Caring Alternatives: Community
      Based Care for the Elderly." THE JOURNAL OF
      SOCIAL ISSUES, 36 (Spring 1980): 133-152.

The institutional-medical model of services for the elderly is examined. The need for an alternative--a set of comprehensive community-based in-home health and social services for the elderly--is substantiated. The legislative framework of Medicare, Medicaid, and Title XX is seen as an inadequate approach to service delivery. Attempts of several states to provide more comprehensive systems are examined. The area of implementing such programs is seen as holding the greatest need for research and policy analysis.

27. Blumenthal, David; Schlesinger, Mark; Drumheller, Pamela B. et al. "Special Report: The Future of Medicare." THE NEW ENGLAND JOURNAL OF MEDICINE, 314 (March 13, 1986). 722-728.

This report summarizes the more important proposals made by the Harvard Medicare Project Study Group. Recommendations are made on reforms directly related to beneficiaries, reforms in payment of physicians, reforms in payments to hospitals, and reforms related to prepaid health care. Costs of the various reforms are projected and time frames for implementation are offered.

28. Bodenheimer, Thomas S. (Institute Study of Labor and Economic Crisis, 131 Townsend Street, San Francisco, CA 941). "Class Contradictions in the Health Care Sector." Paper, Society for the Study of Social Problems at Boston, MA: August 1979.

Medicare and Medicaid caused a massive expansion of the health care sector. However, in the 1960's the author claims that the U.S. capitalist class mounted an attack on the working class to regain its level of profits. Examples of this class struggle are given: the closing of public hospitals, malpractice crises, attempts to control hospital costs, and others.

29. Bowker, Lee H., and Divan, Joan. "Humanization and Organizational Totality in Institutions for the Aged." Paper, Society for the Study of Social Problems, Toronto, Ontario, Canada: August 1981.

30. Brickerfield, Cyril F. "Long-Term Care Solutions
    are Needed Now." AHCA JOURNAL, 11 (October 1985).

31. Brickner, P.W. "Health Care Services for Home-
    bound Aged Maintain Independence, Limit Costs."
    HOSPITAL PROGRAM, 61 (September 1980).

32. Brody, Elaine M., and Brody, Stanley J. "Decade
    of Decision for the Elderly." SOCIAL WORK, 5
    (September 1974): 544-554.

    The role of social work in the field of aging
    is one of advocacy. The advocacy role, to be
    effective, must have hard data to support the
    value commitment of social work which will assure
    that well-being, in addition to longevity and life
    safety, is the societal goal for the aged. These
    data should explore the importance of the family
    as a resource, as well as institutional and
    community services, and should be placed in an
    input-output analysis where cost-effectiveness,
    cost benefit, and social cost are clearly defined.

33. Browne, William P., and Alson, Laura K. AGING AND
    PUBLIC POLICY, Westport, Connecticut: Greenwood
    Press, 1983.

34. Buchanan, Joan, and Mahoney, Charlotte. "Health
    Care and the Elderly: A Promise Broken?" FOCUS
    ON AGING AND THE LAW, 6 (Spring 1985): 4-6.

35. Burney, I.L.; Schieber, G.J.; Blaxall, M.A., and
    Gabel, J.R. "Medicare and Medicaid Physician
    Payment Incentives." HEALTH CARE FINANCING
    REVIEW, 1 (Summer 1979): 62-78.

    Using economic and statistical data, this study
    concludes that Medicare and Medicaid physician
    payment incentives are inconsistent with public
    policy goals.

36. Burns, Eveline M. "The Nation's Health Insurance
    and Health Services Policies." AMERICAN BEHAV-
    IORAL SCIENTIST, 15, 5 (May-June 1972):
    713-732.

The postulate is offered that rising health care
costs and estrangement from the medical profession
have led to greater acceptance of a governmental
role in health care. Medicare and Medicaid are
viewed as part of this reaction.

37. Butler, Robert N. "Mission of the National Institute on Aging." JOURNAL OF THE AMERICAN
GERIATRICS SOCIETY, 251 (March 1977): 97-103.

Discusses the establishment of National
Institute of Aging and its basic purpose and
areas of interest.

38. Califano, Joseph A., Jr. "The Aging of America:
Questions for the Four-Generation Society."
THE ANNALS OF THE AMERICAN ACADEMY OF POLITI-
CAL AND SOCIAL SCIENCE, 438 (July 1978):
96-107.

This is a discussion of problems relative to the
growing population of older people in the United
States. Included among these problems is the
inadequacy of the nation's health and social
service systems that cater to older people.

39. Callahan, J.J., and Wallack, S.S., eds. REFORM-
ING THE LONG TERM CARE SYSTEM. Lexington,
MA: Lexington Books, 1981.

40. Cantwell, J.R. "Copayments and Consumer Search:
Increasing Competition in Medicare and Other
Insured Medical Markets." HEALTH CARE FINANCING
REVIEW, 3 (December 1981): 65-76.

41. Caputi, Marie A., and Heiss William. "THE DRG
REVOLUTION." HEALTH AND SOCIAL WORK, 9
(Winter 1984): 5-12.

42. Carroll, M.S., and Arnett, R.H. "Private Health
Insurance Plans in 1978 and 1979: A Review of
Coverage, Enrollment, and Financial Experience."
HEALTH CARE FINANCING REVIEW, 3 (September
1981): 55-87.

43. Cleverly, William O. "Reimbursement for Capital
    Costs." TOPICS IN HEALTH CARE FINANCING, 6
    (Fall 1979).

44. Cockerham, William C. MEDICAL SOCIOLOGY. Engle-
    wood Cliffs, N.J.: Prentice-Hall Publishing
    Co., 1986.

45. Coe, Rodney M.; Brehm, Henry P.; and Peterson,
    Warren A. "Impact of Medicare on the Organi-
    zation of Community Health Resources." THE
    MILLBANK MEMORIAL FUND QUARTERLY, 52 (Summer
    1974): 231-264.

46. Coelen, C. and Sullivan, D. "An Analysis of the
    Effects of Prospective Reimbursement Programs
    on Hospital Expenditures." HEALTH CARE FINANC-
    ING REVIEW, 2 (Winter 1981): 1-40.

47. Cohen, Toby. "Medicaid Fraud Reconsidered: How
    the Hospitals Got on Welfare." DISSENT, 24
    (Fall 1977): 390-398.

    A discussion of the large shares of income which
    hospitals desire from Medicaid and the shifting of
    overhead costs to outpatient departments. The
    article highlights the insufficient funds to
    investigate cases of mismanagement, fraud, etc.
    Poor administration of the Medicaid program is
    noted.

48. Cohen, Wilbur J. "Reflections on the Enactment
    of Medicare and Medicaid." HEALTH CARE FINAN-
    CING REVIEW, 1985, Annual Supplement: 3-11.

49. Cohen, Wilbur J. "Medicare, Medicaid: 10 Lessons
    Learned." HOSPITALS, 59 (August 1985): 44-47.

50. Cohodes, Donald R. "Hospital Capital Formation
    in the 1980's: Is There a Crisis?" JOURNAL OF
    HEALTH POLITICS, POLICY AND LAW, 8 (Spring
    1983): 164-172.

51. Colombotos, John. "Physicians and Medicare: A
    Before-After Study of the Effects of Legisla-
    tion on Attitudes." AMERICAN SOCIOLOGICAL
    REVIEW, 34 (June 1969): 318-334.

Attitude toward Medicare of New York State
Physicians is studied before and twice after
passage of Medicare into law. The focal question
is, does law influence behavior and attitudes and
act as an instrument of social change? Some laws
may influence attitudes without initially
changing behavior.

52. Commerce Clearing House. MEDICARE AND MEDICAID
    GUIDE. Chicago: Commerce Clearing House, 1981,
    1982, and 1983.

53. Corn, Richard. "The Sensitivity of Prospective
    Hospital Reimbursement to Errors in Patient
    Data." INQUIRY, 18 (Winter 1981): 351-360.

54. Coulton, Claudia, and Frost, Abbiek. "Use of
    Social and Health Services by the Elderly."
    JOURNAL OF HEALTH AND SOCIAL BEHAVIOR, 23
    (December 1981): 330-339.

    Utilizing a large interview sample of persons
    65 years of age and older this study suggests
    that the elderly and the general population are
    similarly affected by need, enabling and predis-
    posing factors in the utilization of health and
    social services.

55. David, S.I. WITH DIGNITY, THE SEARCH FOR MEDICARE
    AND MEDICAID. Westport, CT.: Greenwood Press,
    1985.

56. Davidson, Stephen M. MEDICAID DECISIONS: A
    SYSTEMATIC ANALYSIS OF THE COST PROBLEM.
    Cambridge, MA: Ballinger Publishing Co., 1980.

57. Davidson, Stephen M., and Marmor, Theodore. THE
    COST OF LIVING LONGER: NATIONAL HEALTH
    INSURANCE AND THE ELDERLY. Lexington, MA:
    Lexington Books, 1980.

58. Davis, Karen. "Hospital Costs and the Medicare
    Program." SOCIAL SECURITY BULLETIN, 36
    (August 1973): 18-36.

59. Davis, Karen. "Equal Treatment and Unequal
     Benefits: The Medicare Program." THE MILBANK
     MEMORIAL FUND QUARTERLY, 53 (Fall 1975):
     449-488.

     The distribution of Medicare benefits among the
     elderly is analyzed. Evidence of the differen-
     tials is presented. The effect of health status
     on utilization of medical services by the elderly
     is analyzed. Recommendations are offered for
     reducing differentials in Medicare benefits.
     Policy changes projected to result in a distribu-
     tion of benefits more closely related to health
     care needs of the elderly are indicated.

60. Davis, Karen, et al. "Is Cost Containment
     Working?" HEALTH AFFAIRS, 4 (1985): 81-94.

61. Davis, Karen, and Rowland, Diane. MEDICARE POLICY:
     NEW DIRECTIONS FOR HEALTH AND LONG-TERM CARE.
     Baltimore, MD: John Hopkins Press., 1986.

62. Day, Suzanne Rie. "Home Health Care: The Supply,
     The Demand, and Policy Implications." Paper,
     Society for the Study of Social Problems, New
     York: August 1976.

     The home health delivery system is analyzed to
     determine the nature of barriers to development of
     such care as a major option for ailing older
     adults. One problem relates to internal inconsis-
     tencies in Medicare regulations. The potential
     demand for such care is analyzed through: (1) demo-
     graphic data, (2) data on physical limitations,
     and (3) sociological trends. A proposal is
     offered for research to differentiate among types
     of home-care clients.

63. Deacon, R.W. "Impact of Medicare on the Use of
     Medical Services by Disabled Beneficiaries,
     1972-1974." HEALTH CARE FINANCING REVIEW, 1
     (Fall 1979): 39-54.

This study investigates the impact of the extension of Medicare coverage to disabled persons on
service utilization and costs. Access to care
increased slightly, rate of use did not, and costs
increased.

64. De Friese, Gordon H., and Woomert, Alison. "Self-
    Care Among U.S. Elderly: Recent Developments."
    RESEARCH ON AGING, 5 (March 1983): 3-23.

    In-depth study of 25 self-care activities is
    presented. Descriptive content on the following
    program dimensions is presented: program sponsor-
    ship and setting; target groups; method of program
    implementation; type and size of staff; program
    goals and activities.

65. DeSantis, Grace. "Increasing Access Through In-
    creased Health Manpower: Some Unanticipated
    Effects." Paper, 10th World Congress of the
    International Sociological Association, Mexico
    City: August 1982.

    Traced are the effects of government efforts
    aimed at increasing access to health care in the
    United States. Both the intent of health care
    policy (especially initial legislation enacted
    during the 1960s) and the impact of this legisla-
    tion are examined.

66. Donabedian, Avedis. "Effects of Medicare and
    Medicaid on Access to and Quality of Health
    Care." PUBLIC HEALTH REPORTS, 91 (July-August
    1976): 322-331.

67. Dowd, James J. "Mental Illness and the Aged
    Stranger." INTERNATIONAL JOURNAL OF HEALTH
    SERVICES, 14, 1984: 69-87.

    An attempt is made to: evaluate the dominant
    mental health paradigms within social gerentology;
    synthesize some existing threads of a political
    economy/social control approach to these issues
    and demonstrate that the act of growing old in
    capitalist societies brings increased risk of
    mental illness. The exclusion of the aged from

labor markets and the physical and ideological
"strangeness" of the aged are viewed as primary
factors in disposition toward mental illness of
the elderly.

68. Dunlop, Burton, D.ed. NEW FEDERALISM AND LONG-
    TERM HEALTH CARE OF THE ELDERLY. Milwood, VA:
    Project Hope, 1985.

69. Dunn, Alison. "Growing Old in America." NEW
    SOCIETY, 34 (October 1982): 260-261.

    Until recently, only the wealthiest of the
    senior citizens could escape large health bills
    and expensive private health insurance premiums.
    Medicare and Medicaid reduced some of these
    worries. Due to scandals (involving nursing
    homes, accused of using the welfare programs as a
    means of profit) regulations and inspections have
    become mandatory.

70. Durso, Lori. "Medicare Cost Containment Restrict-
    ing Access to Care, Roybal Says." OLDER
    AMERICAN REPORTS, 9 (July 12, 1985): 3-5.

71. Dutton, B.L., Jr., and McMenamin, P. "The Medi-
    care Economic Index: Its Background and Begin-
    nings." HEALTH CARE FINANCING REVIEW, 3 (Sep-
    tember 1981): 137-140.

72. Eggers, Paul. "Risk Differentiation Between Medi-
    care Beneficiaries Enrolled and Not Enrolled in
    an HMO." HEALTH CARE FINANCING REVIEW, 1
    (Winter 1980): 91-99.

73. Eggers, Paul. "Trends in Medicare Reimbursement
    for End-Stage Renal Disease: 1974-1979." HEALTH
    CARE FINANCING REVIEW, 6 (September 1984): 31-38.

74. Eggers, Paul, and Prihoda, R. "Enrollment Reim-
    bursement Patterns of Medicare Beneficiaries
    Enrolled in 'at risk' HMO's." HEALTH CARE FI-
    NANCING REVIEW, 4 (September 1982): 55-73.

75. Ehrenrich, Barbara, and Enrenrich, John. THE AMERICAN HEALTH EMPIRE. New York: Random House, 1970.

76. Eisdorfer, Carl, et al., eds. ANNUAL REVIEW OF GERONTOLOGY AND GERIATRICS. New York: Springer Publishing Company, 1982.

77. Erskine, Hazel. "The Polls: Health Insurance." THE PUBLIC OPINION QUARTERLY, 39 (Spring 1975), 128-143.

Nine survey organizations have furnished for reprint their previously published findings from polls (between 1936 and 1974) which included health care questions under the following rubrics: (1) voluntary health insurance, (2) medical care for the needy, (3) medical care for the aged, (4) public and private medicare, (5) government medical care, and (6) public versus private health insurance.

78. Estes, Carroll. THE AGING ENTERPRISE. San Francisco, CA: Jossey-Bass, Inc., Publishers, 1979.

79. Estes, Carroll L.; Swan, James H.; and Gerard, Lenore E. "Dominant and Competing Paradigms in Gerontology: Towards a Political Economy of Aging." AGING AND SOCIETY, 2 (July 1982): 151-164.

The origins and influences of social science perspectives have conditioned theoretical and empirical developments in the field of gerontology. Yet, little systematic examination has been applied to the role of social science in the production of knowledge underlying rationales for age-related social policy. Here, dominant U.S. social science paradigms are examined. A proposal is offered for an alternative line of inquiry--a political economy of aging--that includes the effects of social history, world economy, capitalism and social class on the aging process, the aged and the policy interventions designed for them.

80. Estes, Carroll; Newcomer, Robert J., et al.
     FISCAL AUSTERITY AND AGING: SHIFTING GOVERN-
     MENT RESPONSIBILITY FOR THE ELDERLY. Beverly
     Hills, CA: Sage, 1983.

81. Evans, Daryl Paul. "Medical Piecework: The
     Effects of Prospective Payment (DRG's) on Handi-
     capped People." Paper, Western Social Science
     Association Meeting: April 1984.

     This paper assesses the Medicare and Medicaid
     diagnostically related groups reimbursement
     formula. Issues surrounding the formula are
     raised and clarified. Interviews with handicapped
     people report their feelings as to negative
     effects of the policy.

82. Evashwick, C.; Rowe, G.; Diehe, P. and Branch, L.
     "Factors Explaining the Use of Health Care
     Services by the Elderly." HEALTH SERVICES
     RESEARCH, 19 (August 1984): 357-382.

     The Anderson model of health services utiliza-
     tion, including predisposing, enabling and need
     factors, was used to predict utilization for a
     population sample of 1,317 elderly persons. Taken
     alone, the "need" construct was the most important
     single predictor of use of physician services,
     hospitalizations, ambulatory care, and home care.
     "Predisposing" factors were better predictors of
     use of dental services. Multivariate analyses
     demonstrated that the three constructs should be
     applied simultaneously when predicting use of
     services.

83. Eve, Susan Brown. "Age Strata Differences in
     Utilization of Health Care Services Among
     Adults in the United States." SOCIOLOGICAL
     FOCUS, 17 (April 1984): 105-120.

     Differences in access to and use of physicians,
     hospitals, and dentists were examined for three
     age strata (young adults, middle-aged, and older
     adults) using data from 1975 Health Interview
     Survey. Use of physicians and hospitals was
     greatest among older adults. Dentist utilization

was lowest among older adults. Although illness
level was best predictor of use of physicians in
all three strata, other predictors emerged,
including private insurance coverage among older
adults.

84. Falk, I.S. "Medical Care in the U.S.A.--1932-1972.
     Problems, Proposals, and Programs from the Com-
     mittee for National Health Insurance." THE
     MILBANK MEMORIAL FUND QUARTERLY, 51 (Winter
     1973): 1-32.

     An historical review of the background and
     evolution of current medical care. Included is
     an examination of Medicare and Medicaid from
     inception in 1965 to 1972.

85. Falk, I.S. "Proposals for National Health
     Insurance in the U.S.A.: Origins and Evolu-
     tion, and Some Perceptions for the Future."
     THE MILBANK MEMORIAL FUND QUARTERLY, 55
     (Spring 1977), 161-191.

     Described are the origins and evolution of
     National Health Insurance including a discuss-
     ion of the Commission on the Costs of Medical
     Care, the Social Security Act of 1935, and Medi-
     care and Medicaid. Alternatives to the compre-
     hensive National Health Insurance are explored.

86. Feingold, Eugene. MEDICARE: POLICY AND POLITICS.
     San Francisco: Chandler and Sharp Publishers,
     1966.

87. Ferry, T.; Gornick, M., and Newton, M., et al.
     "Physicians' Charges Under Medicare: Assignment
     Rates and Beneficiary Liability." HEALTH CARE
     FINANCING REVIEW, 1 (Winter 1980): 49-73.

88. Fisher, C.R. "Difference by Age Groups in Health
     Care Spending." HEALTH CARE FINANCING REVIEW,
     1 (Spring 1980): 65-90.

89. Fitzmaurice, J.M. "A Statistical Analysis of the
     Medicare Hospital Routine Nursing Salary Cost
     Differential." HEALTH CARE FINANCING REVIEW,
     5 (Fall 1983). 45-64.

90. Fox, Renee C. "The Medicalization and Demedicali-
     zation of American Society." DAEDALUS, 106
     (Winter 1977): 9:22.

91. Freeland, M.S., and Schendler, R.E. "National
     Health Expenditures: Short-Term Outlook and
     Long-Term Projections." HEALTH CARE FINANCING
     REVIEW, 2 (Winter 1981): 97-138.

92. Friedlob, A.S. "Medicare Second Surgical Opinion
     Programs: The Effect of Waiving Cost-Sharing."
     HEALTH CARE FINANCING REVIEW, 4 (September
     1982): 99-106.

93. Galblum, T.W. and Triegen, S. "Demonstration of
     Alternate Delivery Systems Under Medicare and
     Medicaid." HEALTH CARE FINANCING REVIEW, 3
     (March 1982): 1-11.

94. Gibson, R.M., and Fisher, C.R. "Age Differences
     in Health Care Spending, Fiscal Year 1979."
     SOCIAL SECURITY BULLETIN, 42 (1978): 3-16.

95. Gibson, R.M., and Waldo, D.R. "National Health
     Expenditures, 1981." HEALTH CARE FINANCING
     REVIEW, 4 (Summer 1982): 1-35.

96. Gibson, R.M.; Waldo, D.R., and Levit, K.R. "Na-
     tional Health Expenditures, 1982." HEALTH CARE
     FINANCING REVIEW, 5 (Fall 1983): 1-31.

97. Gillick, Muriel R.; Serrell, Nancy A.; and
     Gillick, Laurence S. "Adverse Consequences of
     Hospitalization in the Elderly." SOCIAL SCIENCE
     AND MEDICINE, 16, 1981: 1033-1038.

     This is a longitudinal study of patients under
     and over 70 years of age in terms of consequence
     of hospitalization. The finding is that hospital-
     ized elderly patients are at high risk of
     developing depressed psychophysiologic functioning
     and resultant sustained medical intervention.

98. Gliebe, Werner A. "Unnecessary Educational
     Experimentation: Patients in a Teaching Hospital."
     SOCIOLOGICAL SYMPOSIUM, 23 (Summer 1978): 1-16.

This is an analysis of clinical data concerning
the purpose of each laboratory test ordered by
residents providing patient care. A profile of
the patient most likely to be tested unnecessarily
emerged from the data: patient who enters hospital
without a private physician, nonwhite, female, and
under 65.

99. Goodman, Patsy G. "Ethical Compromises in Long-
Term Care of the Elderly." Paper, Conference on
Humanistic Perspectives on the Aging Enterprise
in America, Kansas City, MO: March 1985.

100. Gornik, Marian. "Ten Years of Medicare: Impact on
the Covered Population." SOCIAL SECURITY
BULLETIN, 39 (July 1976): 3-17.

101. Gornik, Marian. "Trends and Regional Variations
in Hospital Use Under Medicare." HEALTH CARE
FINANCING REVIEW, 3 (March 1982): 41-73.

102. Gornik, Marian; Beebe, J.; and Prihoda, R.
"Options for Change Under Medicare: Impact of a
Cap on Catastrophic Illness Expense." HEALTH
CARE FINANCING REVIEW, 5 (1983): 33-43.

103. Gornik, Marian; Newton, M.; and Hackerman, C.
"Factors Affecting Differences in Medicare
Reimbursement for Physicians Services." HEALTH
CARE FINANCING REVIEW, 1 (Spring 1980): 15-37.

104. Gornik, Marian; Greenberg, Jay; Eggers, Paul; and
Dobson, Allen. "Twenty Years of Medicare and
Medicaid: Covered Populations, Use of Benefits,
and Program Expenditures." HEALTH CARE
FINANCING REVIEW, 1985, Annual Supplement: 13-57.

A comprehensive review of Medicare and Medicaid
data, with an emphasis on beneficiary experiences and
the utilization and costs of services. Also addresses
possible future scenarios.

105. Gottschalk, Shimon S. "Self Help in Health Care: The
Seeds of Change." Paper, Society for the Study of
Social Problems, San Francisco, CA: 1982.

A report of a unique health care service, staffed
entirely by volunteer retired physicians, nurses, and
others, who provide, at little or no cost, for the
health maintenance needs of their aged peers.

106. Grant, Karen R., and Chappell, Neena L. "What Is
Reasonable Is True: Life Satisfaction and Functional Disability Among Day Hospital Participants."

Among several kinds of health care programs enabling the elderly to maintain community residence
is the geriatric day hospital. This study
examines what factors influenced life satisfaction
and functional disability among the elderly
attending three day hospitals in Winnipeg, Canada.

107. Green, Brent. "Internal Colonialism Versus the
Elderly: Renewal and Critique for Gerontological
Theory." BERKELEY JOURNAL OF SOCIOLOGY, 23,
1978-79: 129-150.

Four traditional components of colonization are
discussed, as they provide a framework for the re-
pressive features of old age in free societies.
Included in this discussion is inadequate medical
care. The author contends that Medicaid illus-
trates how the dominant society controls personal
affairs to sustain a "colonized personality."
Ageism is viewed as institutionalized. It is con-
cluded that traditional gerontological theory
ignores socioeconomic and political structures and
overemphasizes psychological and biological
factors.

108. Greenlick, M.R., et al. "Kaiser--Permanente's
Medicare Plus Project: A Successful Medicare
Prospective Payment System for Hospitals." HEALTH
CARE FINANCING REVIEW, 7 (Spring 1986): 97-114.

109. Gutterman, Stuart, and Dobson, Allen. "Impact of
the Medicare Prospective Payment System for Hospitals." HEALTH CARE FINANCING REVIEW, 7
(Spring 1986): 97-114.

110. Hadley, Jack. "How Should Medicare Pay Physicians?" MILBANK MEMORIAL FUND QUARTERLY, 62 (Spring 1984): 279-299.

111. Hall, David, and Bytheway, Bill. "The Blocked Bed: Definition of a Problem." SOCIAL SCIENCE AND MEDICINE, 16, 1982: 1985-1991.

The "blocked bed"--a hospital bed that is unavailable for new admissions because it is occupied by elderly patients unable to return home though not in need of medical care--is widely recognized as a problem of health care in Great Britain but has not been defined clearly.

112. Harrington, Charlene. "Public Policy Issues: The Nursing Home Industry." Paper, Society for the Study of Social Problems, San Francisco, CA: August 1981.

This paper discusses the debate of institution-alization of the aged as a dominant treatment modality. It discusses policy options that limit nursing home admissions, improve quality care, and alternatives that provide health and social services in the home and community.

113. Harrington, Charlene. "Policy Shifts in Social Security and Medicare" in FISCAL AUTHORITY AND AGING by Carroll Estes, Robert S. Newcomer, et al. Beverly Hills, CA: Sage Publication, 1983.

114. Harrington, Charlene; Newcomer, Robert; and Estes, Carroll, et al. PUBLIC POLICY IN LONG TERM CARE. Beverly Hills, CA: Sage, 1984.

115. Harris, Richard. A SACRED TRUST. New York: New American Library, 1966.

116. Harvard Medicare Project. "Medicare: Coming of Age." Cambridge, MA: Center for Health Policy and Management, John F. Kennedy School of Gov-ernment, March, 1986.

117. Hatten, J. "Medicare's Common Denominator: The
     Covered Population." HEALTH CARE FINANCING
     REVIEW, 2 (Fall 1980: 53-64.

118. Heinemann, Gloria D. "Informal Social Support in
     Long-Term Care: Resources or Roadblock?" Paper,
     Society for the Study of Social Problems,
     Toronto, Ontario, Canada: August 1981.

     This paper discusses the research central to the
     issue of the importance of informal social
     supports in the long-term care of the chronically
     ill elderly and what needs to be done in the
     future to clarify the position/role of informal
     supports.

119. Hobart, Helen. "Health Care Costs Containment
     Efforts Ignore Real Problems." OLDER AMERICAN
     REPORTS, 9 (May 24, 1985): 9.

120. Hochbaum, Martin, and Galkin, Florence. "Discharge
     Planning: No Deposit, No Return." SOCIETY, 19
     (January-February 1982): 58-61.

     The discharge planning policies in New York
     nursing homes are scrutinized using 1977/78 data.
     The study suggests that there is little institu-
     tionalized impetus to return patients to their
     homes or to maintain adequate discharge policies.
     At issue: the fact that Medicare does not support
     home health care as it does institutionalized
     care. Recommendations are offered to encourage
     alternative modes of care in communities and to
     stimulate more lawful compliance with discharge
     planning regulations by nursing homes.

121. Hudson, Robert B. "The 'Graying' of the Federal
     Budget and Its Consequences for Old-Age
     Policy." GERONTOLOGIST, 18 (October 1978):
     428-440.

122. Hudson, Robert B., ed. THE AGING IN POLITICS:
     PROCESS AND POLICY. Springfield, IL: Charles
     C. Thomas, Co., 1981.

123. Iglehart, John K. "Medicare Turns to HMO's."
     NEW ENGLAND JOURNAL OF MEDICINE, 312
     (January 10, 1985): 132-136.

124. Illsey, Raymond. "Problems of Dependency Groups:
      The Care of the Elderly, the Handicapped and the
      Chronically Ill." SOCIAL SCIENCE AND MEDICINE,
      15A (June 1981): 327-332.

      The elderly, the handicapped, and the chronical-
      ly ill are considered under the status label of
      "dependency group." Common problems identified
      are: 1) lack of professional interest in their
      medical problem due to inefficacy of treatment; 2)
      costliness due to long-term use of services; 3)
      multiple needs that make single-service accommo-
      dation difficult; 4) low economic productivity and
      socio-economic dependency. Issues of responsibil-
      ity for service to these groups and problems of
      policy implementation are also discussed.

125. Jencks, S.F. and Dobson, A. "Strategies for Re-
      forming Medicare's Physician Payments: Physi-
      cian Diagnosis-Related Groups and Other Ap-
      proaches." NEW ENGLAND JOURNAL OF MEDICINE,
      312 (1985): 1492-1499.

126. Johnson, Allan N., and Appel, Gary L. "DRGs
      and Hospital Case Records: Implications for
      Medical Case Mix Accuracy." INQUIRY, 21
      (Summer 1984): 128-134.

      This study compares Minneapolis-St. Paul area
      hospital records and matching Medicare claim
      records. For the same patient, the DRG based on
      the claim matched the DRG on the medical record
      approximately 50%. The authors conclude that
      hospital case mixes are understated, and DRG
      pricing and hospital reimbursement are affected as
      a result.

127. Johnson, Allan and Aquilina, David. "The Cost
      Shifting Issue." HEALTH AFFAIRS, 1 (Fall 1983):
      103.

128. Johnson, Janet L. and Long, Stephen H. "General
      Revenue Financing of Medicare: Who Will Bear
      the Burden?" HEALTH CARE FINANCING REVIEW, 3
      (March 1982): 13-20.

129. Kane, Robert L., and Kane, Rosalie A. "Care of
      the Aged: Old Problems in Need of New Solutions."
      SCIENCE, 200 (May 26, 1978): 910-919.

130. Kane, Robert; Solomon, David; Beck, John; Keeler,
      Emmett; and Kane, Rosalie. "The Need for Geria-
      tric Manpower in the United States." THE NEW
      ENGLAND JOURNAL OF MEDICINE, 302 (June 1980):
      1327-1332.

131. Kayser-Jones, J.S. "Institutional Structures:
      Catalysts of or Barriers to Quality Care for the
      Institutionalized Aged in Scotland and the
      United States." SOCIAL SCIENCE AND MEDICINE,
      16 (1982): 935-944.

      Through interviews and participant observation,
      the care of the elderly in two long-term care
      institutions, one in Scotland and one in the
      United States, is examined. Catalysts of and
      barriers to quality care are identified. Adequate
      government insurance programs, professional
      specialization in care of aged, and a structure to
      provide on-going comprehensive care are components
      of success. Medicare and Medicaid are viewed as
      barriers to quality care; the National Health
      Service viewed as a catalyst.

132. Keith, Pat M. "Evaluation of Services for the
      Aged by Professionals and the Elderly." THE
      SOCIAL SERVICE REVIEW, 49 (June 1975): 271-278.

133. Keith, Pat M. "Factors Associated with Need:
      Community Health and Social Services Among
      the Aged." JOURNAL OF THE COMMUNITY DEVELOPMENT
      SOCIETY, 9 (Spring 1978): 70-79.

      Studied is the extent to which demographic
      characteristics, attitudes, and life changes ex-
      plain the elderly's perceived needs for community
      services. Elderly interview respondents indicated
      greatest needs were transportation, legal aid, and
      in-home care services. Projected use of services
      had most effect. Variables such as political
      activism by the aged, sex, health evaluation, and

past use had a more limited degree of influence or
perceived needs for community services. Decremen-
tal changes such as loss of health, income, and
ability to participate had no direct effect on the
perceived need for services.

134. Kelsey, Gayleen. "What Does That Old Woman Want
      Now? A Look at the Health Care Providers and
      Aging Women." Paper, New York State Sociolo-
      gical Association Meeting: October 1983.

      The paper discusses the special and multiple
      health needs of the older women and how these are
      reacted to by physicians, hospitals, nurses, and
      the drug industry. A more activist role by older
      women in terms of demanding changes to meet their
      medical needs is suggested.

135. Kennedy, Catherine A.; King, James A.; and Muraco,
      William A. "The Relative Strength of Health as
      a Predictor of Life Satisfaction." INTERNA-
      TIONAL SOCIAL SCIENCE REVIEW, 58 (Spring 1983):
      97-102.

      This is an interview survey of 1200 Ohio resi-
      dents 60 and older. Variables investigated: self-
      assessed health, income, housing, and transporta-
      tion. The findings concur with previous research
      in showing the significant importance of perceived
      health as the strongest predictor of life satis-
      faction of the elderly. Income, housing, and
      transportation are viewed as indirectly affecting
      contentment via perceived health.

136. Kinkead, Brian M. "Medicare Payment and Hospital
      Capital: Future Policy Options." HEALTH AFFAIRS
      (Fall 1984): 35.

137. Kinney, Eleanor D., and Lefkowitz, Bonnie. "Capi-
      tal Cost Reimbursement to Community Hospitals
      Under Federal Health Insurance Programs." JOUR-
      NAL OF HEALTH POLITICS, POLICY AND LAW, 7
      (Fall 1982): 648-666.

138. Klarman, Herbert E. "Major Public Initiatives in
      Health Care." THE PUBLIC INTEREST, 34
      (Winter 1974): 106-123.

This article examines increases in health care
expenditures. The time period covered is 1950-1972.
Most of the increase in cost followed the imple-
mentation of Medicare and Medicaid in 1966.
Models of explanation for cost increases are
examined. New programs, i.e., Regional Medical
Programs, Comprehensive Health Planning, and Health
Maintenance Organizations are also discussed.

139. Kraus, A.S.; Spasoff, R.A.; Beattie, E.J.;
      Holden, D.E.W.; Lawson, J.S.; Rodenburg, M.;
      and Woodcock, G.M. "Elderly Applicants to
      Long-Term Care Institutions, II. The Appli-
      cation Process, Placement and Care Needs."
      JOURNAL OF THE AMERICAN GERIATRICS SOCIETY,
      24 (April 1976): 165-172.

      The process of applying for long-term care
      institutions, which includes motivations, choice
      of institution, and attitudes and expectations, is
      studied in the cases of 193 applicants. More than
      50% of applicants and about 80% of their family
      members approved of the proposed move. The number
      applying to homes for the aged opposed to other
      institutions seemed much greater than appropriate;
      many of these applicants appeared more eligible
      for placement in foster homes and specialized
      facilities for the demented or for remaining in
      their own homes. About 20% of applicants could
      have continued living independently if they had
      received reasonable community assistance.

140. Kruse, Thomas L. "Government vs. The Private
      Sector: Health Care for the Elderly." Paper,
      Society for the Study of Social Problems, New
      York: August 1986.

141. Kruse, Thomas L. "Medicare Policy: Its Effects
      on Human Services." Paper, Society for the Study
      of Social Problems, Washington, D.C.: August 1985.

142. Kronenfeld, Jennie J. "Has the Medicaid Program
      Led to Equal Tratment in Health Care?" SOCIOLO-
      GICAL FORUM, 1 (Fall 1978): 46-59.

The Medicaid program is seen as having been
somewhat successful in equalizing utilization of
physicians' services. This article questions,
however, whether the program has also equalized
the kinds of sources from which people derive
health care services. Certain population groups
have distinctive patterns of obtaining care,
despite equalization in use of services. Speci-
fically, blacks, low-income people, and people
receiving Medicaid are likelier to name places
rather than individual physicians as health care
sources.

143. Kronenfeld, Jennie J. "The Provision of Health
     Care Services to the Poor: Medicaid, State Dif-
     ferences, and Policy Suggestions of the Reagan
     Administration." Paper, Society for the Study
     of Social Problems, San Francisco, CA: August 1982.

     This paper investigates the Medicaid program and
     the implications of federal and state budgetary
     changes as enacted in 1981. It describes these
     changes enacted in fiscal 1982 and how six states
     are responding to cutbacks; the possible implica-
     tions of these cutbacks and the "New Federalism"
     proposal for 1984 are discussed.

144. Krout, John A. "The Rural Elderly: Issues in Ser-
     vice Provisions and Utilization." Paper, The
     Rural Sociological Society, San Francisco, CA:
     August 1982.

     This paper reviews available research re: defi-
     cient services available to rural elderly as
     compared to urban counterparts. It discusses the
     implications for rural aged service programs and
     policy.

145. Kutner, Nancy G. "Cost-Benefit Issues in Nation-
     al Health Legislation: The Case of the End-
     Stage Renal Disease Program." Paper, Society
     for the Study of Social Problems, San Francisco,
     CA: August 1982.

This paper discusses the difficulty of implementing cost containment in treatment of catastrophic injury or illness. Medicare funding for
treatment of end-stage renal disease represents an
experiment in federal financing for medical intervention in catastrophic illness. Third-party
reimbursement and the vested interests of
physicians are explored as are factors affecting
the program's costs.

146. Lammers, William W. PUBLIC POLICY AND THE AGING.
     Washington, D.C.: C. Q. Press, 1983.

147. Landsberger, Henry A. "The Underlying Dimensions
     of Health Policy: A Cross-National Study of
     Health Policy Elites and of Students in the
     Health Professions. "Paper, World Congress of
     the International Sociological Association,
     Mexico City: August 1982.

     The paper discusses health policy questions
     applicable to countries with very different struc-
     tures for the delivery of health care. Empirical
     data from the U.S. and West Germany are presented.

148. Lee, Philip R. "Health Policy Issues for the
     Aged: Challenges for the 1980's." GENERATIONS,
     4 (May 1980): 38-40, 73.

149. Lee, Philip R. "Public Policies, The Aged and
     Long-Term Care." JOURNAL OF LONG-TERM CARE AD-
     MINISTRATION, 7 (Fall 1979): 1-15.

150. Lee, Phillip R.; Estes, Carroll L.; LeRoy, Lauren;
     and Newcomer, Robert. "Health Policy and the
     Aged." ANNUAL REVIEW OF GERONTOLOGY AND GERIA-
     TRICS, 3, 1982: 361-400, edited by Carl Eisdor-
     fer, et al., New York: Spring Publishing
     Company.

     This chapter is a review of research findings
     and data in terms of how they can be applied to
     policy decisions that affect the health care of
     the aged. There is an examination of the chang-
     ing conceptions of aging, ageism, and health. The
     authors contend that factors other than health

care, e.g., biology, life style, and environment,
determine health and suggest criteria for policy
and action. The costs of health care for the
elderly are documented. Emphasis is on the need
for new organizational structures to deliver
health care to the elderly, on pre-paid plans such
as H.M.O.'s for the elderly and on controlling
costs through competitive market forces.

151.   Levine, Eugene, and Abdellah, Faye G. "DRGs: A
       Recent Refinement to an Old Method." INQUIRY,
       21 (Summer 1984): 105-112.

       The DRG classification system is not without
       historical antecedent. The authors trace its his-
       torical roots.

152.   Levitt, L. "The Crisis in Social Security and
       Medicare." JOURNAL OF JEWISH COMMUNAL SERVICE,
       60 (1983): 112-119.

       The future financial stability of Medicare is
       discussed in terms of impact on the Jewish commu-
       nity and the community's evaluation of health
       care. It is asserted that Medicare financing must
       be isolated from the problem of unemployment if
       continuity and predictability of programming are
       to continue.

153.   Link, C.R.; Long, S.H.; and Settle, R.F. "Cost
       Sharing, Supplementary Insurance, and Health
       Services Utilization Among the Medicare
       Elderly." HEALTH CARE FINANCING REVIEW, 2
       (Fall 1980): 25-31.

       This is an investigation of the extent to which
       private supplementary insurance and Medicaid
       encourage the elderly to seek additional health
       care. The authors conclude that private or public
       supplements to Medicare induce greater use of
       health services.

154.   Linn, Bernard S., and Linn, Margaret W. "Objec-
       tive and Self-Assessed Health in the Old and

56   **MEDICARE**

Very Old." SOCIAL SCIENCE AND MEDICINE, 14
(July 1980): 311-315.

155. Lipman, Aaron, and Largino, Charles F., Jr. "Formal and Informal Support: A Conceptual Clarifi-
cation." JOURNAL OF APPLIED GERONTOLOGY, 1
(June 1981): 141-146.

Means of formal and informal support for the
elderly are functionally differentiated. While
these two types of support are interrelated, each
functions most effectively in specific areas.
Formal support operates within the context of
bureaucractic structure, reflecting both its
strengths and limitations. Formal organizations,
however, could never hope to meet all of the
instrumental, social, and emotional needs of the
individual. The mechanisms by which formal
agencies supplement informal support deserve much
greater attention in applied gerontological
research.

156. Long, S.H., and Settle, R.F. "Medicare and the
Disadvantaged Elderly: Objectives and Outcomes."
MILBANK MEMORIAL FUND QUARTERLY/HEALTH AND
SOCIETY, 62 (1984): 609-656.

The authors see the major objectives of Medicare
to improve access to health care services for the
most disadvantaged elderly by removing barriers of
distribution, attitude, and finance. They see the
program as generally successful but claim that
some problems of access remain and some costly
side effects exist.

157. Long, S.H., and Skitter, R.F. "Equity and
Medicare: Evidence for Vulnerable Elderly Sub-
populations." Paper, American Public Health
Association, Montreal, Canada: November 1982.

158. Long, S.H. and Skitter, R.F. "Medicare Cost Shar-
ing and Private Supplementary Health Insurance:
Selected Research Findings." Paper, American
Public Health Association, Montreal, Canada:
November, 1982.

159. Lowenstein, Regina. "Early Effects of Medicare on the Health Care of the Aged." SOCIAL SECURITY BULLETIN, 34 (April 1971): 3-20.

160. Lowry, Louis. SOCIAL POLICIES AND PROGRAMS ON AGING. Lexington, MA: Lexington Books: 1980.

161. Lubitz, Jim, and Prihoda, Ronald. "The Use and Costs of Medicare Services in the Last Two Years of Life." HEALTH CARE FINANCE REVIEW, 5 (Spring 1984): 117-131.

162. Luft, Harold S. "Medical Care in a Changing Economic Environment." THE PHAROS, (Winter 1985): 2-5.

163. McAuley, William J., and Arling, Greg. "Use of In-Home Care by Very Old People." JOURNAL OF HEALTH AND SOCIAL BEHAVIOR, 25 (March 1984): 54-64.

Three questions related to use of in-home care by persons aged 75 and over are addressed: 1) is there a hierarchy of types of care received in home? 2) can the number of in-home services received be explained by the background characteristics, mental or physical status, or level of functional impairment of the individual? 3) what factors distinguished users of formal services from those who rely exclusively on informal services? Findings indicate a hierarchy of need. Use of formal services is more likely among persons who are better educated, live in urban areas, are in better condition regarding instrumental activities of daily living, and whose day-to-day problems are more physical.

164. McCall, Nelda. "Utilization of Medicare Services by Beneficiaries Having Partial Medicare Coverage." HEALTH CARE FINANCING REVIEW, 5 (Winter 1983): 35-49.

165. McMillan, Alma; Pine, Penelope; Gornick, Marion; and Prihoda, Ronald. "A Study of the 'Crossover Population': Aged Persons Entitled to Both Medicare and Medicaid." HEALTH CARE FINANCING REVIEW, 4 (Summer 1983): 19-46.

166. Maddox, George L., and Dellinger, David C.
     "Assessment of Functional Status in a Program
     Evaluation and Resource Allocation Model." THE
     ANNALS OF THE AMERICAN ACADEMY OF POLITICAL AND
     SOCIAL SCIENCE, 438 (July 1978): 59-70.

167. Marmor, Theodore R. THE POLITICS OF MEDICARE.
     Chicago: Aldine, 1973.

168. Marmor, Theodore R. "Varieties of American Health
     Politics." Paper, 10th World Congress of the
     International Sociological Association, Mexico
     City: August 1982.

     There are various federal policies that affect
     health that are not health policies per se.
     Federal action consists of a multitude of programs
     with differing histories, politics, goals, and
     results. This paper looks at health policy in
     light of politics at the onset of the 1960s, the
     health agenda was dominated by the politics of
     expansion, but in 1980, the politics of scarcity
     dominated.

169. Marmor, Theodore R. "Why Medicare Helped Raise
     Doctor's Fees." TRANSACTION, 5 (September
     1968): 14-19.

170. Master, Robert J.; Feltin, Marie; Jainchill, John;
     Mark, Roger; Kanesh, William; Rabkin, Mitchell;
     Turner, Barbara; Bachrach, Sarah; and Lennox,
     Sara. "A Continuum of Care for the Inner City:
     Assessment of its Benefits for Boston's Elderly
     and High-Risk Populations." THE NEW ENGLAND
     JOURNAL OF MEDICINE, 302 (June 26, 1980:
     1434-1440.

     Described is an approach to health care in the
     inner city: a multi-disciplinary system of physi-
     cians and mid-level practitioners that provides in-
     stitutionalized care to chronically ill, elderly,
     homebound, and nursing home residents of Boston.

171. Matthews, Sarah H. "Negotiation by Default: The
     Social Definition of Old Widows." Paper,
     Society for Study of Social Problems, Chicago,
     IL: August 1977.

Social definition of the old is traced back from
the Social Security Administration and Medicare,
to the date of publication. The old, however, define themselves as middle-aged and capable of
dealing with their own lives. A clash between the
definitions is explored. A plea is made for put-
ting money into the pockets of the old rather than
the pockets of middlepersons so that the old will
have power to construct their own realities.

172. Merritt, R.E., and Potemken, D.B., eds. MEDIGAP:
ISSUES AND UPDATE. Washington, D.C.: The
Intergovernmental Health Policy Project, George
Washington University, 1982.

173. Miller, Dulcy B.; Lowenstein, Regina; and Winston,
Ricky. "Physicians' Attitudes Toward the Ill
Aged and Nursing Homes." JOURNAL OF THE AMERI-
CAN GERIATRICS SOCIETY, 24 (November 1976):
498-505.

A survey of physicians in private practice in
the White Plains, N.Y., area was conducted to
determine whether their attitudes toward the ill
aged and nursing homes were predictors of the
quality of medical care available to area nursing
home patients. The findings demonstrate general-
ized medical disinterest in the care of ill aged
patients in institutions.

174. Minkler, Meredith. "Blaming the Aged Victim: The
Politics of Scapegoating in Times of Fiscal Con-
servatism." INTERNATIONAL JOURNAL OF HEALTH
SERVICES, 13 (January 1983): 155-168.

Scapegoating is examined, particularly with
regard to how it has been directed at the elderly
in the United States. Several contexts are presented within which recent budget cuts affecting
the elderly may be viewed, and showing how the
aged have been blamed for the current fiscal
crisis. The victims of the 60s and early 70s,
"the elderly," were defined as a social problem
and solutions (e.g., increased social security
benefits, Medicare, Medicaid) were devised for
dealing with problems. However, the victim

blaming of the 1980s defines these earlier "solutions" as part of the problem. Education grounded
in political-economic analyses of the "aging-
problem," aimed in part at overcoming structurally
induced divisiveness among oppressed groups, is
suggested as an important deterrent to the
increased polarization that the current fiscal
crisis mentality has nurtured.

175.   Mitchell, Janet B. and Cromwell, Jerry.   "Impact
       of All-Or-Nothing Assignment Requirements Under
       Medicare."   HEALTH CARE FINANCING REVIEW, 4
       (Summer 1983): 59-78.

176.   Montgomery, Rhonda Voight.   "Care Practices in
       Long-Term Care Facilities: The Impact on
       Residents, Family and Staff."   Paper, Midwest
       Sociological Society, Minneapolis, MN:
       April 1979.

       This paper assesses the current individual-
       acute model of care and practices relative to
       people in long-term care.   It discusses an
       alternative model: "family oriented long-term."
       Three theoretical frameworks from social science
       are reviewed in terms of policy recommendations
       for program design and implementation: exchange
       theory, family stress theory, and balance
       theory.

177.   Morgan, David L.   "Failing Health and the Desire
       for Independence: Two Conflicting Aspects of
       Health Care in Old Age."   SOCIAL PROBLEMS,
       30 (October 1982): 40-50.

       Interviews with residents and the staff of an
       old home reveal conflict between the two groups
       over differences in perception of the costs and
       benefits of moving from semi-independent apart-
       ments to a nursing area.   Residents expect low
       medical gains and high social losses from this
       type of move; staff expects the opposite.

178.   Muse, D.N. and Sawyer, D.   THE MEDICARE AND MEDI-
       CAID DATA BOOK, 1981.   Washington, D.C.: United
       States Health Care Financing Administration,
       Office of Research and Demonstration, 1982.

179. Myers, Robert J. MEDICARE. Homewood, IL: Irwin
     Press, 1970.

180. Myles, John F. "Institutionalization and Sick
     Role Identification Among the Elderly." AMERI-
     CAN SOCIOLOGICAL REVIEW, 43 (August 1978):
     508-521.

     Contrary to the hypothesis tested, the institu-
     tionalized elderly are less likely than the nonin-
     stitutionialized elderly to incorporate the
     illness label into their self-definitions.

181. National Health Center for Health Statistics,
     Health Services, and Mental Health Administra-
     tion. "Age Patterns in Medical Care, Illness
     and Disability." VITAL AND HEALTH STATISTICS,
     Series 10, No. 70 (April 1972): 1-88.

     This is a report on age patterns with emphasis
     on persons over sixty-five and the use of medical
     services, illness, and disability during the post-
     Medicare period Jan. 1968-Dec. 1969. The data
     were compared with those from a previous study to
     examine changes which might have resulted from
     Medicare legislation.

182. National Center for Health Statistics, Health Ser-
     vices, and Mental Health Administration.
     "Changes for Care and Sources of Payment for
     Residents in Nursing Homes." VITAL AND HEALTH
     STATISTICS, Series 12, No. 21 (July 1973): 1-69.

     Monthly charges for care in nursing homes in the
     United States during June-August, 1969, are
     examined and analyzed for payment sources for that
     care. Charges in 1969 were significantly higher
     than in 1964. Most of the residents (93%) paid
     for their care from their own or their family's
     income or received Medicare or Medicaid, other
     public assistance, or welfare.

183. National Center for Health Statistics, Health
     Services, and Mental Health Administration.
     "Nursing Homes: Their Admission Policies,

62

MEDICARE

Admissions and Discharges: United States,
April - Sept. 1968." VITAL AND HEALTH STATIS-
TICS, Series 12, No. 16 (December 1972): 1-63.

Introduction by Jeannine Fox Sutton. Data col-
lected in the 1968 Nursing Home Survey as
presented: number of residents, admissions, discharges, admission policies, monthly charges for
care, number and kinds of employees, and medical
and recreational services offered. This survey is
compared with the Resident Places Survey-1 of
1963. The number of homes, beds and residents in
personal care homes where nursing (intermediate
level) has decreased since 1963, while the number
of homes, beds and residents in homes providing
nursing care (highest level of nursing service)
has increased.

184. National Center for Health Statistics, Health
      Services, and Mental Health Administration.
      "Services and Activities Offered to Nursing
      Home Residents." VITAL AND HEALTH STATISTICS,
      Series 12, No. 17 (December 1972): 1-42.

This report deals with rehabilitation services,
medical care, and recreational activities offered
by nursing homes in the United States in 1968.

185. Newcomer, Robert, et al. "Medicare Prospective
      Payment: Anticipating Effect on Hospitals,
      Other Community Agencies and Families."
      JOURNAL OF HEALTH POLITICS, POLICY AND LAW,
      10 (1985): 275-282.

186. Newcomer, Robert J., and Harrington, Charlene A.
      "State Health and Human Service Policies and
      Their Influence on Long-Term Care Patient
      Placements and Transfer." Paper, Society for
      the Study of Social Problems, San Francisco, CA:
      August 1982.

This paper discusses the utilization patterns of
eight state health and human service departments
that provide services to persons sixty-five and
over. It covers the period 1978-1981. State

Medicaid and social services policies are described and compared for their influence on the
utilization of long-term care services.

187.   Newman, Howard N. "Medicare and Medicaid." ANNALS
       OF THE AMERICAN ACADEMY OF POLITICAL AND SOCIAL
       SCIENCE, 299 (January 1972): 114-124.

       Medicare and Medicaid are viewed as a new kind
       of federal commitment to health care. The author
       claims that both programs were designed to operate
       within the existing health care system, but no
       provisions were made for expanded services.
       Concern must be shown for improving the system.
       Possible future forms of federal involvement in
       health care are discussed. The author cautions
       that whatever new forms arise, financing and
       provision of services must be addressed more
       adequately.

188.   Newman, Sandra J. "Governmental Policy and the
       Relationship Between Adult Children and Their
       Aging Parents: Filial Support, Medicare, and
       Medicaid." Paper, Gerontological Society, San
       Diego, CA: November 1980.

189.   O'Sullivan, Jennifer. MEDICARE: FY 1987 BUDGET.
       Washington, D.C.: Congressional Research Ser-
       vices, 1987.

190.   O'Sullivan, Jennifer. MEDICARE PHYSICIAN PAY-
       MENTS. Washington, D.C.: Congressional Research
       Services, 1986.

191.   Olson, Laura K. THE POLITICAL ECONOMY OF AGING:
       THE STATE, PRIVATE POWER AND SOCIAL WELFARE.
       New York: Columbia University Press, 1982.

192.   Palley, Howard A., and Palley, Marian Lief. "The
       Determination of Pricing Policy in the Health
       Care Delivery System." AMERICAN BEHAVIORAL
       SCIENTIST, 19 (September 1975): 104-121.

       A review is presented of the interactions
       between public and private sectors in health care
       pricing particularly with regard to Medicare.

Because the public sector was largely unorganized
and the private sector highly organized, the
latter has been more dominant than the former.

193. Paringer, L. "Medicare Assignment Rates of Physi-
     cians: Their Responses to Changes in Reimburse-
     ment Policy." HEALTH CARE FINANCING REVIEW, 1
     (Winter 1979): 75-89.

194. Pearman, William A. "Costs Versus Care--Issues in
     Health Care Through The Life Cycle." Paper,
     Society for the Study of Social Problems, New
     York: August 1986.

195. Pearman, William A. "An Overview of the Develop-
     ment of Medicare Policy: Issues Over Time."
     Paper, Society for the Study of Social Problems,
     Washington, D.C.: August 1985.

196. Pegels, Carol C. HEALTH CARE AND THE ELDERLY.
     Gaithersburg, MD: Aspen Systems, 1980.

197. Pettengill, Julian. Medicare: THE FINANCING
     PROBLEM IN THE HOSPITAL INSURANCE PROGRAM.
     Washington, D.C.: Congressional Research
     Services, 1986.

198. Pettengill, Julian. "Trends in Hospital Use by
     the Aged." SOCIAL SECURITY BULLETIN, 35
     (July 1972): 3-15.

199. Pine, P.L.; Gornick, M.; Lubitz, J.; and Newton,
     M. "Analysis of Services Received Under Medi-
     care by Specialty of Physician." HEALTH CARE
     FINANCING REVIEW, 3 (September 1981): 89-116.

Physicians in general practice and in internal
medicine are most commonly used by Medicare recipients. There are marked geographic differences
in the use of medical specialists, but 85% of
beneficiaries saw primary care physicians and 15%
saw specialists. Interesting is the fact that 20%
of Medicare reimbursement went to internists and
only 15% to general practitioners. Also, it is
reported that 21% of the gross income of
internists comes from Medicare.

200. Piore, Nora; Lieberman, Purlaine; and Linnane,
     James. "Public Expenditures and Private Con-
     trol? Health Care Dilemmas in New York City."
     THE MILBANK MEMORIAL FUND QUARTERLY, 55
     (Winter 1977): 79-116.

     New York City's attempt to transform traditional
     welfare medical care arrangements into an
     integrated, equitable health care system raises
     cautionary signals for rational policy. The
     effects of the Social Security Amendments of 1965
     are examined; as are the changes brought about in
     the access of the old and poor to hospital and
     physician services. Priorities in health spending
     are analyzed. The benefits and problems in the
     decade following introduction of Medicare and
     Medicaid are discussed.

201. Poen, Monte M. HARRY S. TRUMAN VERSUS THE MEDICAL
     LOBBY: THE GENESIS OF MEDICARE. Columbia, MO:
     University of Missouri Press, 1979.

202. Pratt, Henry J. THE GRAY LOBBY. Chicago: Univer-
     sity of Chicago Press, 1976.

203. Puglisi, J. Thomas; Patnaik, Beverly; McCoy,
     William J.; and Begole, Jane A. "A Needs
     Assessment of Older Persons." JOURNAL OF
     APPLIED GERONTOLOGY, 2 (December 1983): 116-118.

204. Ransen, David L. "Some Determinants of Decline
     Among the Institutionalized Aged: Overcare."
     THE CORNELL JOURNAL OF SOCIAL RELATIONS, 13
     (Summer 1978): 61-74.

205. Reamer, Frederic G. "Facing Up to the Challenge
     of DRG's." HEALTH AND SOCIAL WORK, 10
     (Spring 1985): 85-94.

206. Reinhardt, Uwe E. "Hard Choices in Health Care: A
     Matter of Ethics" in HEALTH CARE: HOW TO
     IMPROVE IT AND PAY FOR IT. Washington, D.C.
     Center for National Policy, 1985.

207. Rice, Dorothy P., and Feldman, Jacob J. "Living
      Longer in the United States: Demographic Changes
      and Health Needs of the Elderly." MILBANK
      MEMORIAL FUND QUARTERLY/HEALTH AND SOCIETY, 61
      (Summer 1983): 362-396.

      The field of gerontology seeks to preserve the
      integrity and efficiency of human beings into
      older age. However, knowledge of aging,
      especially healthy aging, remains limited. In
      recent years, a new gerontology has begun to
      emerge. The literature of this new approach is
      briefly reviewed. The problems of extending the
      life span, preserving quality of life, adapting
      society to these achievements appear solvable. A
      research agenda is outlined for gerontology based
      on these concerns.

208. Rice, Dorothy P., and Wilson, Douglas. "The
      American Medical Economy: Problems and Perspec-
      tives." JOURNAL OF HEALTH POLITICS, POLICY AND
      LAW, 1 (Summer 1976): 151-172.

      Medicare and Medicaid have introduced large
      amounts of money into the American medical system
      and have improved health care access for the poor
      and aged. At the same time, third party payment
      mechanisms have increased costs of hospital care
      and specialized medical services. This has
      produced questions concerning the value of medical
      care in improving health. The authors recommend
      reorganizing health care toward a rational use of
      resources.

209. Rice, Thomas, and McCall, Nelda. "Changes in
      Medical Reimbursement in Colorado: Impact on
      Physician's Economic Behavior." HEALTH CARE
      FINANCING REVIEW, 3 (June 1982): 67-85.

210. Rich, Bennett M., and Baum, Martha. THE AGING:
      A GUIDE TO PUBLIC POLICY. Pittsburgh: Univer-
      sity of Pittsburgh Press, 1984.

211. Richmond, H.; Weltzner, J., and Farrow, F., eds.
      "Public Policies for Long Term Care." Chicago:
      University of Chicago Press, 1981.

212. Ritter, Christian, and Taylor, Gregory S. "Satis-
      faction with Health Services Among the Elderly
      and Non-elderly: A Comparison of Two Path
      Models." Paper, The Mid-South Sociological Asso-
      ciation, Little Rock, AR: October 1980.

      Compared are different casual models for
      individuals under and over age sixty-five to
      assess how well each model predicts utilization
      and satisfaction with health services. Three
      general components in the models are predisposing
      factors, enabling factors, and illness level as
      measured by overall satisfaction with one's
      health. Data are based on a state-wide mailed
      survey in Kentucky.

213. Roth, Julius A. "A Catalog of State Cost Contain-
      ment Measures with Commentary." RESEARCH IN THE
      SOCIOLOGY OF HEALTH CARE (1984): 1-8.

      The items in a report by the California Center
      for Health Statistics "Medi-Cal Program
      Highlights" from 1969-1979 are reclassified and
      summarized to show the kinds of measures state
      government agencies have applied to contain the
      costs of the Medicaid program. In addition to
      summarizing the nature of governmental action,
      each category is accompanied by comments on its
      relative success in containing costs.

214. Rovner, Julie. "Long-Term Care: The True 'Catas-
      trophe'?" CONGRESSIONAL QUARTERLY WEEKLY
      REPORT, 44 (May 31, 1986): 1227-1231.

215. Rubin, Robert J., and Helms, Robert B. "Medicare
      Payment of Hospital Capital-Related Costs."
      HEALTH CARE FINANCIAL MANAGEMENT, 38 (April
      1984): 21-28.

216. Ruther, Martin, and Dobson, Allen. "Equal Treat-
      ment and Unequal Benefits: A Re-examination of
      the Use of Medicare Services by Race: 1967-1976."
      HEALTH CARE FINANCING REVIEW, 2 (Winter 1981):
      55-83.

217. Saward, Ernest W. "The Organization of Medical
     Care" in LIFE, DEATH, AND MEDICINE, San Fran-
     cisco: W.H. Freeman and Company, Publishers,
     1973: 129-135.

218. Scanlon, William J. "Nursing Home Utilization
     Patterns: Implications for Policy." JOURNAL
     OF HEALTH POLITICS, POLICY, AND LAW, 4 (Winter
     1980): 619-641.

     This is a review of research on nursing home
     utilization with regard to several policy issues
     concerning the subsidization of long-term care by
     Medicaid: 1) defines and contrasts need, demand,
     and utilization; 2) indicates how Medicaid's
     policies regarding reimbursement and eligibility
     can result in chronic shortage of beds; 3) de-
     scribes estimated effects on utilization of eight
     variables--Medicaid generosity, age structures,
     family resources, racial composition, residence,
     financial capability of elderly, price of nursing
     home care, and alternative sources of care.

219. Schieber, George J.; Burney, Ira L.; Golden,
     Judith B.; and Knaus, William A. "Physician
     Fee Patterns Under Medicare: A Descriptive
     Analysis." THE NEW ENGLAND JOURNAL OF MEDI-
     CINE, 294 (May 1976): 1089-1093.

     Physician reimbursement practices by carriers
     under the Medicare program are described for both
     the claims payment process and the determination
     of reasonable charges. Discretionary practices,
     which may differ among carriers and which may
     affect the survey results, are noted. Information
     was received for 292 reasonable charge localities.
     Results indicate that the maximum prevailing
     charge for each procedure generally ranges from
     three to ten times the minimum charge.

220. Schwartz, Joel J., and Tabb, David. "Social Wel-
     fare: Changing Policies and Changing Priori-
     ties." AMERICAN BEHAVIORAL SCIENTIST, 15
     (May-June 1972): 645-664.

This article examines social welfare policy of
the late 1960s. The political environment of the
late 60s is viewed as a factor in the rise of
social welfare spending. The authors contend that
welfare spending advantages those groups with the
least need. The authors contend that changes in
the late 60s in Medicare and Medicaid increased
the cost burden of health services for the elderly
and poor.

221. Shulman, David, and Galanter, Ruth. "Reorganizing
      the Nursing Home Industry: A Proposal." THE
      MILBANK MEMORIAL FUND QUARTERLY, 54 (Spring
      1976): 129-163.

      Under the nursing home industry's organizational
      pattern, owners have a financial incentive to
      maximize capital costs and minimize operating
      costs, to gain a nontaxable cash flow that is as
      large as possible. Under an alternative system,
      in which capital facilities are owned by
      governments and management carried out by private
      contractors, this problem could be avoided;
      operators would not be preoccupied with capital
      values, and periodic renewal of contracts would
      make review of operations automatic, insuring
      quality control.

222. Simborg, Donald W. "DRG Creep: A New Hospital
      Acquired Disease." NEW ENGLAND JOURNAL OF MEDI-
      CINE, 304 (June 25, 1981): 1602-1604.

223. Skelton, David. "The Future of Health Care for
      the Elderly." JOURNAL OF THE AMERICAN GERIA-
      TRICS SOCIETY, 25 (January 1977): 39-46.

      The major future requirements in health care for
      the elderly are outlined and widely supported by
      other practitioners in the field. Suggested are
      the following: increased education in the
      disciplines of gerontology and geriatric medicine,
      increased societal awareness of the realities of
      aging, better communication and teamwork among
      health care professionals, greater coordination of
      health care delivery system components, greater
      emphasis on research into changing and evaluating

needs of elderly health care recipients, and
emphasis on prevention and early detection of
disease.

224. Snider, Earle L. "Factors Influencing Health
     Service Knowledge Among the Elderly." JOURNAL
     OF HEALTH AND SOCIAL BEHAVIOR, 21 (December
     1980): 371-377.

225. Snider, Earle L. "The Role of Kin in Meeting
     Health Care Needs of the Elderly." CANADIAN
     JOURNAL OF SOCIOLOGY, 6 (Summer 1981): 325-336.

226. Snider, Earle L. "Social Indicators, Health
     Policy, and the Elderly." SOCIAL INDICATORS
     RESEARCH, 11 (November 1982): 405-419.

227. Social Legislation Information Service. "HCFA
     Issues Trend Data on Medicare Enrollment."
     WASHINGTON SOCIAL LEGISLATION BULLETIN, 29
     (March 11, 1985).

228. Somers, Anne R. "Long-Term Care for the Elderly
     and Disabled: A New Health Priority." THE NEW
     ENGLAND JOURNAL OF MEDICINE, 307 (July 1981):
     221-226.

     A discussion of problems and policies
     surrounding the issue of long-term health care for
     the elderly and chronically ill is presented. The
     failure of policies is outlined, and a possible
     solution involving both Medicare and Title XXI of
     the Social Security Act is proposed.

229. Sommers, Herman M., and Sommers, Anne R. MEDICARE
     AND THE HOSPITALS: ISSUES AND PROSPECTS. Wash-
     ington, D.C.: Brookings Institute, 1967.

230. Sotdo, Beth T., and Manton, Kenneth. "Health
     Status and Service Needs of the Oldest Old:
     Current Patterns and Future Trends." MILBANK
     MEMORIAL FUND QUARTERLY/HEALTH AND SOCIETY, 63
     (Spring 1985): 286-319.

231. Starr, Paul. THE SOCIAL TRANSFORMATION OF AMERI-
     CAN MEDICINE. New York: Basic Books, 1982.

232. Stevens, Rosemary. AMERICAN MEDICINE AND THE
     PUBLIC INTEREST. New Haven: Yale University
     Press, 1971.

233. Stojanovic, Elisabeth J. "The Dissemination of
     Information About Medicare to Low Income Rural
     Residents." RURAL SOCIOLOGY, 37 (June 1972):
     253-260.

     This study addresses the sources of information
     about Medicare for low-income women in rural
     sections of the southeastern United States. It
     also looks at the extent of the women's
     information about Medicare and their participation
     in the program. The best source of information
     was radio and television, but the lowest social
     class was least likely to be reached by these
     media forms. Other potential sources of informa-
     tion dissemination, e.g., extension services or
     churches, are suggested.

234. Stevens, Robert, and Stevens, Rosemary. WELFARE
     MEDICINE IN AMERICA: A CASE STUDY OF MEDICAID.
     New York: Free Press, 1974.

235. Stewart, William. "The Positive Impact of Medi-
     care on the Nation's Health Care Systems."
     SOCIAL SECURITY BULLETIN, 30 (July 1967): 9-12.

236. Stoesz, David. "Corporate Health Care and Social
     Welfare." HEALTH AND SOCIAL WORK, 11 (Summer
     1986): 165-172.

237. Sundquist, James L. POLITICS AND POLICY: THE
     EISENHOWER, KENNEDY AND JOHNSON YEARS. Wash-
     ington, D.C.: The Brookings Institute, 1968.

238. Thompson, Frank J. HEALTH POLICY AND THE BUREAU-
     CRACY. Cambridge, MA: M.I.T. Press, 1981.

239. U.S. Department of Health, Education and Welfare.
     Social Security Administration. BACKGROUND ON
     MEDICARE 1957-1962: REPORTS, STUDIES AND CON-
     GRESSIONAL CONSIDERATIONS ON HEALTH LEGISLATION.
     85th-87th Congress, 2 Vols., Washington, D.C.:
     Government Printing Office, 1963.

240. U.S. Department of Health and Human Services. Health
     Care Financing Administration. HEALTH MAINTENANCE
     ORGANIZATIONS AND MEDICARE. Washington, D.C.:
     U.S. Government Printing Office: March 1982.

241. U.S. Department of Health and Human Services.
     Health Care Financing Administration. TEN YEARS
     OF SHORT-STAY HOSPITAL UTILIZATION AND COSTS
     UNDER MEDICARE, 1967-1976. Washington, D.C.:
     Health Care Financing Administration, Office of
     Research, Demonstrations, and Statistics:
     August 1980.

242. U.S. Department of Health and Human Services.
     Office of the Assistant Secretary for Planning
     and Evaluation. HOSPITAL CAPITAL EXPENSES:
     A MEDICARE PAYMENT STRATEGY FOR THE FUTURE.
     Washington, D.C.: U.S. Government Printing
     Office: March 1986.

243. U.S. Department of Health and Human Services.
     Office of the Inspector General. CAPITAL COST
     ISSUES THAT NEED TO BE ADDRESSED IN DEVELOPING
     MEDICARE REIMBURSEMENT POLICY. Washington,
     D.C.: U.S. Government Printing Office: May 1985.

244. U.S. Department of Health and Human Services.
     Office of the Secretary. "Hospital Prospective
     Payment for Medicine." Report to Congress, in
     MEDICARE AND MEDICAID GUIDE, 374 (January 1983),
     Chicago: Commerce Clearing House, Inc., 1983.

245. U.S. Department of Health and Human Services.
     Social Security Administration. YOUR RIGHT TO
     APPEAL DECISIONS ON HOSPITAL INSURANCE CLAIMS:
     January 1983.

246. U.S. Department of Health and Human Services.
     Social Security Administration. YOUR RIGHT TO
     APPEAL YOUR MEDICAL INSURANCE PAYMENT. August
     1981.

247. General Accounting Office. HISTORY OF THE RISING
     COSTS OF MEDICARE AND MEDICAID PROGRAMS AND
     ATTEMPTS TO CONTROL THESE COSTS, 1966-1975.
     Washington, D.C.: U.S. Government Printing
     Office, 1977.

248. U.S. General Accounting Office. Report of the Comptroller General of the United States to the Congress. HOME-HEALTH--THE NEED FOR A NATIONAL POLICY TO BETTER PROVIDE FOR THE ELDERLY. Washington, D.C.: U.S. General Accounting Office: December 1977.

249. U.S. General Accounting Office. RISING HOSPITAL COSTS CAN BE RESTRAINED BY REGULATING PAYMENTS AND IMPROVING MANAGEMENT. Washington, D.C.: U.S. General Accounting Office, 1980.

250. U.S. General Accounting Office. HEALTH CARE FACILITIES: CAPITAL CONSTRUCTION EXPENDITURES BY STATE. Washington, D.C.: U.S. General Accounting Office: August 1986.

251. U.S. General Accounting Office. IMPAIRED KNOWLEDGE BASE WOULD BE HELPFUL IN REACHING POLICY DECISIONS ON PROVIDING LONG-TERM, IN-HOME SERVICES FOR THE ELDERLY. Washington, D.C.: U.S. General Accounting Office: December 1981.

252. U.S. General Accounting Office. Report to the Chairman, Subcommittee on Health, Committee on Ways and Means, House of Representatives. MEDICARE: ALTERNATIVES FOR PAYING HOSPITAL CAPITAL COSTS. Washington, D.C.: Government Printing Office: August 1986.

253. U.S. General Accounting Office. Report of Subcommittee on Intergovernmental Relations and Human Resources, Committee on Government Operation. AN AGING SOCIETY: MEETING THE NEEDS OF THE ELDERLY WHILE RESPONDING TO RISING FEDERAL COSTS. Washington, D.C.: U.S. General Accounting Office: September 1986.

254. U.S. House of Representatives. Select Committee on Aging. AMERICA'S ELDERLY AT RISK. Washington, D.C.: U.S. Government Printing Office, 1985.

255. U.S. House of Representatives. Select Committee
     on Aging. THE ATTEMPTED DISMANTLING OF THE
     MEDICARE HOME CARE BENEFIT. Washington, D.C.:
     U.S. Government Printing Office: April 1986.

256. U.S. House of Representatives. Select Committee
     on Aging. CATASTROPHIC HEALTH INSURANCE: THE
     'MEDIGAP' CRISIS. Washington, D.C.: U.S. Gov-
     ernment Printing Office: August 1986.

257. U.S. House of Representatives. Select Committee
     on Aging. CONTINUING CARE: INTERNATIONAL
     PROTOTYPES FOR AMERICA'S AGED. Washington,
     D.C.: U.S. Government Printing Office: July 1985.

258. U.S. House of Representatives. Select Committee
     on Aging. HEALTH CARE COST CONTAINMENT: ARE
     AMERICA'S AGED PROTECTED? Washington, D.C.:
     U.S. Government Printing Office: July 1985.

259. U.S. House of Representatives. Select Committee
     on Aging. HOME HEALTH CARE: THE ARIZONA PER-
     SPECTIVE. Washington, D.C.: U.S. Government
     Printing Office: May 1986.

260. U.S. House of Representatives. Select Committee
     on Aging. MEDICARE AND MEDICAID REFORM: PRO-
     TECTING THE AGED AND INDIGENT IN TEXAS. Wash-
     ington, D.C.: U.S. Government Printing Office:
     July 1985.

261. U.S. House of Representatives. Select Committee
     on Aging. MEDICARE OPTIONS FOR 1985. Washing-
     ton, D.C.: Government Printing Office: January
     1985.

262. U.S. House of Representatives. Select Committee
     on Aging. TWENTIETH ANNIVERSARY OF MEDICARE
     AND MEDICAID: AMERICANS STILL AT RISK. Wash-
     ington, D.C.: U.S. Government Printing Office:
     July 1986.

263. U.S. House of Representatives. Select Committee
     on Aging. Report of the Chairman, AMERICA'S

UNINSURED AND UNDERINSURED: A NATION AT RISK OF
INADEQUATE HEALTH CARE AND CATASTROPHIC COSTS.
Washington, D.C.: U.S. Government Printing
Office, September 1986.

264. U.S. National Commission on Social Security
      Reform. REPORT OF THE NATIONAL COMMISSION ON
      SOCIAL SECURITY REFORM. Washington, D.C.:
      U.S. Government Printing Office: January 1983.

265. U.S. Office of the Inspector General. MEDICARE
      HOME HEALTH SERVICE: A SERVICE DELIVERY ASSESS-
      MENT. Washington, D.C.: U.S. Government
      Printing Office: November 1981.

266. U.S. Public Law 97-35. OMNIBUS BUDGET RECONCIL-
      IATION ACT OF 1982. (H.R. 3982). Amendments
      to Title XXI--Medicare, Medicaid, Section 2100,
      passed by Congress, July 31, 1981. Washington,
      D.C.: U.S. Government Printing Office, 1981.

267. U.S. Senate. Special Committee on Aging. HEALTH
      CARE EXPENDITURES FOR THE ELDERLY: HOW MUCH
      PROTECTION DOES MEDICARE PROVIDE? Washington,
      D.C.: U.S. Government Printing Office, 1982.

268. U.S. Senate Special Committee on Aging. MEDICARE
      AND THE HEALTH COSTS OF OLDER AMERICANS: THE
      EXTENT AND EFFECTS OF COST SHARING. Washington,
      D.C.: U.S. Government Printing Office, 1984.

269. U.S. Senate. Special Committee on Aging, Subcom-
      mittee on Long Term Care and on Health of the
      Elderly. JOINT HEARINGS: MEDICARE AND MEDICAID
      FRAUDS. Washington, D.C.: U.S. Government
      Printing Office, 1976.

270. Van den Heunel, W.J.A. "The Concept of Health in
      the Elderly." Paper, World Congress of Inter-
      national Sociological Association, Mexico City:
      August 1982.

271. Vogel, R.J., and Palmer, H.C. LONG TERM CARE:
      PERSPECTIVES FROM RESEARCH AND DEMONSTRATIONS.
      Rockville, MD: Aspen Systems Corporation, 1985.

272. Waldo, Daniel R., and Lanzeby, Helen C. "Demo-
      graphic Characteristics and Health Care Use
      and Expenditures by the Aged in the United
      States: 1977-1984." HEALTH CARE FINANCING
      REVIEW, 6 (September 1984): 1-29.

273. Wales, Jeffrey B. "The Ethics of Research with
      Aged Human Subjects." Paper, American Socio-
      logical Association, New York: August 1980.

274. Wan, Thomas T.H., and Odell, Barbara Gill.
      "Factors Affecting the Use of Social and
      Health Services Among the Elderly." AGING
      AND SOCIETY, 1 (March 1981): 95-115.

      This study examines the use of health and social
      services among noninstitutionalized elderly, ac-
      cording to Andersen's and Newman's model. Need
      for services was the most important predictor of
      use of physician services and hospitalization.
      Predisposing factors had the most effect on use of
      dental services. Knowledge of services, an
      enabling factor, was most relevant to use of
      social services. Several program strategies are
      suggested for increasing awareness of social
      services, particularly among the impaired elderly.

275. Wan, Thomas T.H., and Arling, Gregg. "Differen-
      tial Use of Health Services Among Disabled
      Elderly." RESEARCH ON AGING, 5 (September
      1983): 411-431.

      This study reports on a survey of elderly resi-
      dents of Virginia who have one or more limiting
      chronic conditions. The purpose is to identify
      variables related to use of ambulatory services.
      Psychological as opposed to medical needs are
      noted as contributing to a large number of visits
      to the doctor.

276. Ward, Russell A. "Services for Older People:
      An Integrated Framework for Research."
      JOURNAL OF HEALTH AND SOCIAL BEHAVIOR, 18
      (March 1977): 61-70.

Conceptual approaches to the study of health
care utilization furnish a useful framework within
which to integrate recent gerontological research
and utilization data. Three factors from selected
findings are discussed: 1) predisposing factors,
2) enabling factors, and 3) illness levels. Use
of this approach helps make discussion of past
results and future research needs, regarding both
the aged and health care utilization, more
coherent, and policy implications may become more
apparent. The model itself is improved by
studying older people as a special utilization
case and by broadening its applicability to
include social services as well as health
services.

277. Wattenberg, Shirley H., and McGann, Leona M.
      "Medicare or 'Medigap'? Dilemma for the
      Elderly." HEALTH AND SOCIAL WORK, 9 (Summer
      1984): 229-237.

      The authors discuss how bureaucratic problems
      associated with Medicare and supplemental
      insurance work to the detriment of the elderly.
      Often elderly do not know of their entitlement or
      are not able to fill out claim forms. Policy
      implications for social workers and health service
      personnel are discussed.

278. Weil, Peter A. "Comparative Costs to the Medicare
      Program of Seven Prepaid Group Practices and
      Controls." THE MILBANK MEMORIAL FUND QUARTERLY,
      54, (Summer 1976): 339-365.

      The costs to the Medicare program of providing
      health care to old people through prepaid group
      practice are compared with those of open market
      health care. The greatest cost savings to the
      Medicare program are with groups that are small
      and hospital based.

279. Wildavsky, Aaron. "Doing Better and Feeling
      Worse: The Political Pathology of Health
      Policy." DAEDALUS, 106 (Winter 1977): 105-123.

Most Americans seem to feel that they receive
good medical care, but that medical care is in
crisis. The paradox rises from many factors, the
most basic of which is the "great equation":
medical care equals health. Health becomes
equivalent to access to medical care, which
affects the quantity but not necessarily the
quality of medical care. How can medical care
which is personalized and yet "free" be provided
without the problems of overcrowding and crushing
tax burdens? Discussed are: Medicare, Medicaid,
NHC's, HMO's, CHIP, and the Kennedy-Mills Proposal.

280. Wildemer, Geraldine, et al. "Home Health Care--
      Services and Cost." NURSING OUTLOOK, 26
      (August 1978).

281. Wohl, S. THE MEDICAL-INDUSTRIAL COMPLEX. New
      York: Harmony Books, 1984.

282. Wolinsky, Frederic D.; Coe, Rodney M.; Miller,
      Douglas K.; Prendergast, John M.; Creel, Myra
      J.; and Chavaz, M. Noel. "Health Service Utili-
      zation among the Noninstitutionalized Elderly."
      JOURNAL OF HEALTH AND SOCIAL BEHAVIOR, 24
      (December 1983): 325-337.

      This study of noninstitutionalized elderly
      residents of St. Louis assesses the effects of
      predisposing, enabling, and need characteristics
      on measure of health care utilization. Need
      characteristics explain much variance in health
      service utilization. The authors suggest that
      this underscores equity in our health care system.
      Nutritional risk is viewed as the most important
      indicator of doctor, emergency rooms, and hospital
      visits.

283. Wolkstein, Irwin. "Medicare 1971: Changing Atti-
      tudes and Changing Legislation." LAW AND CON-
      TEMPORARY PROBLEMS, 35 (Autumn 1970): 697-715.

      This article reviews H.R.I., a social security
      bill that passed the House of Representatives in
      1971. The proposal is seen as a symbol of dissat-

isfaction with Medicare and as a forerunner of new health care delivery guidelines. Medicare reimbursement is the focus. More coverage but also more cost control is the substance of the proposal.

284. Young, Karen M., and Fisher, Charles R. "Medicare Episodes of Illness: A Study of Hospital, Skilled Nursing Facility, and Home Health Agency Care." HEALTH CARE FINANCING REVIEW, 2 (Fall 1980): 1-24.

285. Zubkof, M.; Raskin, I.; and Hanft, R. (eds.) HOSPITAL COST CONTAINMENT. New York: Prodist, 1978.

286. Zweck, Brad. "Hospital Cost Increases Hit 20 Year Low." OLDER AMERICAN REPORTS, (April 26, 1985): 5.

287. Zweck, Brad. "Reagan Medicare Policy Stirs Access, Quality Questions." OLDER AMERICAN REPORTS, 9 (March 1, 1985): 5-6.

288. Zweck, Brad. "Trustees' Report Doesn't Alter for Medicare Need for Medicare Cuts: Heckler." OLDER AMERICAN REPORTS, 9 (April 5, 1985): 5.

January 3, 1965   "DIRKSON MAY BACK US AID TO SCHOOLS".
                   Sen. E. Dirkson unlikely to end opposition
                   to Medicare. (p.45)
                   "NEW PAYROLL TAX URGED FOR HOSPITAL
                   CARE FOR AGED".
                   Government Advisory Council on Social
                   Security proposes separate payroll tax as
                   part of Social Security System for hospital
                   care of aged. (p.68)

January 5   "TRANSCRIPT OF THE PRESIDENT'S
                   MESSAGE TO CONGRESS ON THE STATE
                   OF THE   UNION."
                   President Johnson, as part of the State of
                   the Union message, urges Congress to pass
                   Medicare bill. (p.16)

January 8   "JOHNSON   HEALTH   PROGRAM   GIVES
                   MEDICARE   PRIORITY;   REGIONAL   CENTERS
                   SOUGHT."
                   President Johnson gives first priority to
                   Medicare to be financed through special
                   trust fund under Social Security System.
                   (p.1)

January 10   "NEW HEALTH PLAN OFFERED BY AMA."
                   AMA proposes insurance plan for needy
                   aged which utilizes Blue Cross-Blue Shield
                   and the use of governmental funds for
                   those unable to pay the insurance. (p.1)
                   "BEHIND THE MEDICARE PROGRAM."
                   History of and problems involved in
                   Medicare is reviewed with graphs showing
                   growth in the number of elderly,
                   percentage of elderly prone to major
                   illness, cost of hospital care for the
                   elderly increasing and median income of
                   the elderly decreasing. (D, p.6)

January 26   "MEDICARE ACTIONS BEGINS TOMORROW."
                   Congressman W. Mills sets work on
                   Medicare bill for 1/27. (p.14)

January 26	"TEXT OF PRESIDENT'S MESSAGE AND AN ANALYSIS OF FEDERAL BUDGET."
	President Johnson backs Medicare in budget message that proposes substantial rise in Social Security Taxes to pay for Medicare. (p.25)
January 28	"HOUSE HEARINGS OPEN ON MEDICARE."
	House of Representatives Committee begins work on Medicare with Secretary of Health, Education and Welfare Calabreeze presenting administration case. (p.14)
January 29	"G.O.P. OFFERS A MEDICARE PLAN BASED ON VOLUNTARY PREMIUMS."
	Congressmen Byrnes, Ford, and four other Republicans introduce bill calling for comprehensive care for aged. (p.13)
February 7	"DOCTORS QUESTION MEDICARE STAND."
	AMA House of Delegates endorses own plan and opposes Medicare as proposed by President Johnson. (p.57)
February 16	"AMA QUESTIONS MEDICARE FUNDS."
	AMA and chief actuary R.J. Myers for Social Security differ as to whether Myers projections should lead one to conclude that the Social Security System would go bankrupt in 10 years if Medicare were enacted. (p.21)
February 17	"PRESIDENT URGES PUBLIC TO PRESS MEDICARE ACTION."
	President Johnson asks general public to urge prompt enactment of Medicare bill. (p.1)
February 23	"MEDICARE PROGRAM SCORED BY DENTAL GROUPS' LEADER."
	ADA joins AMA in opposing Medicare bill; urges strengthening of Kerr–Mills Act. (p.27)
February 24	"LABOR CHIEFS WARN OF FIGHT BY AMA."
	AFL–CIO Executive council endorses Medicare bill. (p.1)

March 6   "HOUSE PANEL DUE TO ADD COVERAGE TO MEDICARE PLAN."
House of Representatives Committee nears passage of enlarged Medicare bill; Doctors' fees, drugs and other medical services are added to hospitalization as covered items. Expansion offered by Congressman J.W. Byrnes. (p.1)

March 24   "EXPANDED MEDICARE BILL IS VOTED BY HOUSE PANEL."
House of Representatives Ways and Means Committee approves expanded version of Administration's Medicare bill; President Johnson pleased. (p.1)

March 25   "MEDICARE'S PROGRESS."
Congressman W. Mills support for the bill, after 7 years of opposition, seen as chief factor in Way and Means passage of Medicare bill. (p.49)

April 1   "MEDICARE PUSHED IN HOUSE."
Eight Republicans on Ways and Means Committee say Medicare bill enactment would threaten Social Security System. (p.14)

April 7   "HOUSE DEBATES MEDICARE TODAY."
House of Representatives Rules Committee clears Medicare bill for vote by full house by 10 to 5 vote. (p.1)

April 9   "HOUSE APPROVES MEDICARE, 313-115: GOP PLAN LOSES."
House of Representatives, 313-115, passes administration Medicare bill; President Johnson hails passage. (p.1)
"MAJOR PROVISIONS OF THE MEDICARE BILL."
Major provisions of the bill and roll call vote of House of Representatives detailed. (p.16)

April 11   "THE MEDICARE BILL."
Dr. H. Rusk of Rehabilitation Institute endorses Medicare bill. (p.95)

84

May 1   "LONG BIDS SENATE WIDEN MEDICARE."
         Senate Committee begins hearings on
         Medicare. Senator R. B. Long opposes bill
         because it doesn't deal with catastrophic
         illness. (p.11)
May 11   "INSURERS SCORE A MEDICARE PLAN."
         M. Eddy, President of American Health
         Insurance Association, predicts the
         enactment of Medicare will drive private
         insurance companies out of business.
         (p.13)
May 12   "AMA HEAD SEES DECLINE IN CARE."
         AMA President says Medicare bill will lead
         to decline in quality of medical care.
         (p.21)
May 17   "AMA LEADER HITS MEDICARE."
         AMA president-elect alleges that the real
         purpose of the Medicare bill is to
         federalize U.S. hospitals. (p.28)
May 19   LONG INTRODUCES NEW HEALTH PLAN."
         Senator Long introduces a substitute bill
         and its provisions are detailed. (p.23)
June 9   "AMA CRITICIZES MEDICARE IN AD."
         AMA initiates ad campaign against
         Medicare saying that it will lead to
         socialized medicine. (p.25)
June 18 "MEDICARE REVISED TO HELP THE POOR."
         Senate Finance Committee adopts Senator
         Long's amendments shifting Medicare from
         limited benefits for all aged to
         unrestricted benefits mainly for the poor.
         (p.1)
June 21 "NEW AMA CHIEF WARNS AGAINST
         MEDICARE BOYCOTT."
         AMA chief urges doctors not to boycott
         Medicare if enacted. (p.1)
June 24 "SENATE UNIT KILLS MEDICARE CHANGES."
         Senate Finance Committee reverses itself;
         deletes Long amendments; pressure by
         President Johnson resulted in reversal
         vote. (p.1)
June 25 "MEDICARE VOTED BY SENATE PANEL."
         Senate Finance Committee passes Medicare
         bill in almost identical shape as House of
         Representatives passed bill. (p.20)

June 25   "AMA PROPOSES MEDICARE TALKS."
AMA resolutions reject Medicare boycott as official policy. (p.1)

July 7   "MEDICARE DEBATE OPENS IN SENATE."
United States Senate opens debate on Medicare bill. (p.21)

July 10   "SENATE PASSES MEDICARE BILL BY VOTE OF 68-21."
Senate passes Medicare bill which goes to Conference Committee to resolve differences between two bills. (p.1)

July 22   "CONFEREES CLEAR BILL ON MEDICARE."
Congressional Conference approves final text of Medicare bill calling for expansion of Social Security system to provide hospitalization, nursing home care, home nursing services, and outpatient diagnostic services to all Americans over 65; supplementary federal insurance to cover doctor bills at premium cost of $ 3.00 per month; law to take effect 7/1/66. (p.1)

July 28   "MEDICAL AID BILL VOTED BY HOUSE."
House of Representatives approves Medicare bill, 307 to 116. (p.18)

July 29   "CONGRESS PASSES BILL ON MEDICARE."
Senate approves Medicare bill, 70 to 24. (p.14)

July 31   "PRESIDENT SIGNS MEDICARE BILL."
President Johnson signs Medicare bill into law in Independence, Missouri to salute former President Truman's call for Medicare-like bill in 1945. (p.1)

August 2   "PERSONAL FINANCE: IMPACT OF MEDICARE."
Economic impact of Medicare is discussed. (p.35)

August 5   "MEDICARE BOYCOTT URGED FOR DOCTORS."
The members of the Association of American Physicians and Surgeons are urged to boycott Medicare program. (p.1)

August 12   "MEDICARE CAUTION GIVEN PHYSICIANS."
AMA states that individual members can boycott Medicare but cannot act in concert via association. (p.15)

86

August 14	"DOCTORS' GROUP SAYS AMA AIDS 'EVIL.'" Association of American Physicians and Surgeons criticize AMA stand. (p.20)
September 1	"U.S. MAILING KITS ON HEALTH PLANS." Federal government begins mailing Medicare information kits and application forms to 15.5 million persons over 65. (p.1)
September 9	"VOLUNTARY MEDICARE ENROLLS FIRST MEMBER." T. Palcorolla, 68, is the first to enroll in Medicare at White House; President Johnson urges all eligible to sign up. (p.23)
October 12	"MEDICARE PAYMENTS STUDIES." Advisory Committee at Social Security headquarters to weigh how to reimburse hospitals under Medicare. (p.30)
October 30	"DR. FISHBEIN SAYS CONDITIONS CHANGE, HE IS FOR MEDICARE." Dr. M. Fishbein, former President of AMA, now backs Medicare due to changing conditions; formerly opposed it. (p.27)
November 8	"U.S. BRIEFS HOSPITALS ON MEDICARE INTERMEDIARIES." Social Security administration details how hospitals may pick intermediary to handle payment of patient bills; growing dispute over procedures noted. (p.25)
November 13	"BLUE CROSS NOMINATED MEDICARE INTERMEDIARY." American Hospital Association nominates Blue Cross to be administrative intermediary under Medicare. (p.25)
November 26	"AMA ASSISTING MEDICARE PLANS." AMA President Appel urges all doctors to cooperate with Medicare to assure that the blame for the harmful effects of bill will fall on the government and not on the medical community. (p.39)
December 6	"PERSONAL FINANCE: HOPES FOR MEDICARE PROGRAM." Medicare aims and provisions are discussed. (p.59)

December 13	"DOCTORS ADJUSTING TO MEDICARE, BUT ONE THORNY ISSUE REMAINS." AMA and government work quietly together on compromises on Medicare. (p.24)
December 28	"U.S. TO ALERT THE ELDERLY TO THEIR MEDICARE RIGHTS." Office of Economic Opportunity to finance projects to let people know of their Medicare rights. (p.12)
March 9, 1966	"MEDICARE FUNDS WILL BE USED TO SPUR RIGHTS ACT IN HOSPITALS." PHS to use Medicare funds to effect compliance with 1964 Civil Rights Act barring racial discrimination by any institution getting federal aid. (p.26)
May 8	"255 AREAS IGNORE PUPIL BIAS PLEDGE." As part of press conference, Secretary of Health, Education and Welfare Gardner stated that his department is doing everything possible to secure compliance by hospitals with the Civil Rights Act. (p.22)
May 16	"MEDICARE 'CRISIS' CITED BY KENNEDY." Senator Robert F. Kennedy says he will introduce a bill to commit the federal government to spend $2 billion in 10 years to meet national "crisis" in facilities for the elderly on the eve of the start of Medicare. (p.1)
May 22	"HOSPITAL ASSOCIATION URGES COMPLIANCE WITH RIGHTS ACT." American Hospital Association delegates urged all hospitals to comply with Civil Rights Act ban on racial discrimination. (p.42)
May 25	"U.S. AWAITS PLEDGES BY 1,000 HOSPITALS." The government reports that 1,000 hospitals, mostly in South, have not qualified to participate in Medicare. (p.49)

88

May 26	"MEDICARE FACING CIVIL RIGHTS SNAG." Health, Education, Welfare department engaged in crash program to achieve compliance by Southern hospitals before Medicare takes effect. (p.40)
June 5	"U.S. CUTS MORE AID TO SOUTH SCHOOLS: 18 AREAS AFFECTED." Most hospitals in Georgia are not in compliance with Civil Rights Act raising questions about Medicare program. (p.79)
June 16	"PRESIDENT URGES MEDICARE SUPPORT." President Johnson urges White House Conference on Medicare to focus on hospitals' preparedness for the number of expected patients. (p.1)
July 1	"MEDICARE: HOW THE ELDERLY PATIENT GETS BENEFITS." Article describes how elderly persons use Medicare card to obtain benefits. (p.1) "MORE HOSPITALS COMPLY ON RIGHTS." Health, Education, Welfare reports that 92% of the hospitals are in compliance with the Civil Rights Act in order to participate in Medicare program. (p.16)
August 19	"DOCTORS' FEES UP AS MUCH AS 300% UNDER MEDICARE." New York City doctors raise fees for aged as much as 300% since Medicare began 7/1/66. (p.1)
August 24	"U.S. PLANS INQUIRY INTO MEDICAL COSTS UP 3.4% THIS YEAR." President Johnson orders Secretary Gardner of Health, Education, Welfare to begin a "major study" of rising medical costs. (p.1)
September 6	"HOSPITAL RATES IN U.S. INCREASING FIVE TIMES FASTER THAN COST OF LIVING." Survey shows hospital bills rose at 5 times cost of living in sixties; higher pay is a factor as well as cost of sophisticated equipment. (p.1)

September 28   "SENATE RESTRICTS RIGHTS GUIDELINES."
                 U.S. Senate, in a surprise 55 to 11 vote,
                 permits segregated hospital rooms in
                 certain cases. (p.23)

October 22   "CAMPAIGN TAX AID HELD UP IN SENATE."
                 H o u s e   s t r i k e s   f r o m
                 Health,Education,Welfare appropriation bill
                 Senate amendment permitting segregated
                 hospital rooms. (p.20)

December 23   "DIP IN FOOD PRICES HOLDS COSTS RISE
                 TO 6-MONTH LOW."
                 Medical care services continue spectacular
                 rise in costs as compared to overall index.
                 (p.1)

January 5, 1967 "U.S. DECIDES AGAINST ENFORCING
                 MEDICARE LOYALTY OATH PROVISION."
                 Justice Department concedes that Medicare
                 loyalty oath is unconstitutional when memo
                 is filed with Superior Court. (p.26)
                 "ADA FOR TAX RISE TO PAY FOR GAINS."
                 Americans for Democratic Action urges
                 prepaid health insurance for all under
                 Social Security. (p.26)

January 24   "TEXT OF PRESIDENT JOHNSON'S SPECIAL
                 MESSAGE TO CONGRESS ON AID FOR THE
                 ELDERLY."
                 President Johnson's message on older
                 Americans urges Medicare extension in
                 various areas. (p.16)

February 14   "NON-RED DISCLAIMER BARRED IN
                 MEDICARE."
                 U.S. Supreme Court, following Justice
                 Department move, rules Medicare loyalty
                 oath unconstitutional. (p.47)

February 25   "TEACHERS' MEDICARE BACKED"
                 Senator Ribicoff offers bill to extend
                 Medicare to 689,000 teachers not covered
                 by Social Security. (p.13)

March 9   "COSTS MAY FORCE MEDICARE TAX RISE."
                 Congressman Mills says rising hospital
                 costs may force Congress to seek more tax
                 revenues to keep Medicare program in
                 black. Others testify on escalating costs.
                 (p.30)

March 23	"REUTHER ASSAILS MEDICARE BILLING." UAW Reuther sees many retired people worse off under Medicare because doctors bill patients directly instead of accepting direct payment from government. Urges changes in Medicare. (p.71)
April 5	"AMA ASKS CONGRESS NOT TO EXPAND MEDICARE." House of Representatives Committee receives testimony on Johnson's plan to extend Medicare coverage. (p.43)
May 2	"MEDICARE SHARE CALLED LOW." American Hospital Association says that its 6,700 hospitals may end Medicare practice unless government pays higher share of costs. (p.56)
June 15	"MEDICARE BILLS PAID IN 3 WEEKS." Commissioner Ball assesses the first year of Medicare's operation. Says program has improved and prolonged life of aged; segregation of many hospitals ends. (p.49)
June 25	"MEDICARE: THE RECORD AT ONE." Review article on Medicare's first year appears in Section D. (p.6)
June 26	"THREE MEDICAL GROUPS EXCORIATE AMA" New AMA President Rouse objects to direct billing of services for payments on Medicare to the government. (p.13)
July 2	"PARTY GOVERNORS SHIFT ON JOHNSON." President Johnson lauds Medicare successes and deplores refusal by some doctors to participate. (p.16)
July 2	"HEALTH INSURERS DISCOVER A NEW FRIEND – MEDICARE." Services on Medicare's first year illustrating its boom effect on nursing homes and greater opportunity for profits for insurance companies. Section C. (p.1)
July 23	"HOUSE UNIT BACKS RISE IN TAX RATES ON AGED BENEFITS." House of Representatives Committee tentatively agrees to raise Social Security rates to make up for higher Medicare costs. (p.1)

August 3   "HOUSE UNIT BACKS 12 1/2% PENSION
                  RISE."
                  House of Representatives Committee
                  extends hospital coverage from 90 to 120
                  days limit; Patient will pay one half of the
                  cost for the additional 30 days. (p.22)

August 18   "HOUSE VOTES 12 1/2% PENSION RISE AND
                  TIGHTENS CURBS ON WELFARE."
                  By a 415-3 vote, House of Representatives
                  passes bill amending Social Security law
                  that liberalizes Medicare program. (p.1)

August 29   "STANDARD SCHEDULE OF MEDICARE FEES
                  OPPOSED BY AMA."
                  In Senate hearing of bill passed by House
                  of Representatives, AMA opposes any move
                  to establish a standardized Medicare fee
                  schedule. (p.25)

October 1   "MEDICARE FEE LIMIT URGED."
                  In testimony before Senate Committee,
                  National Senior Citizens Council urges
                  ceilings on fees doctors charge for
                  treating Medicare patients; protests
                  outrageous escalation of fees. (p.49)

October 25   "MEDICARE'S FIRST YEAR: U.S. REPORTS
                  PROGRAM PAID OUT $3.2 BILLION TO
                  COVER DOCTOR AND HOSPITAL BILLS."
                  Report on first year of Medicare's
                  operation made at American Public Health
                  Association Meeting. (p.28)

October 26   "SENATE DECLINES TO CURB SPENDING."
                  Medicare payments, contribute to record
                  non-defense transfer payments recorded by
                  federal government. (p.30)

November 2   "SENATE PANEL VOTES INCREASE OF 15%
                  IN SOCIAL SECURITY BENEFITS."
                  Senate Committee votes to reject President
                  Johnson's proposal to provide Medicare
                  coverage for 1.5 million disabled workers
                  under 65. (p.34)

November 30   "AMA SEEKS DATA ON MEDICARE COSTS."
                  AMA House of Delegates requests the
                  federal government to release
                  administrative costs as they believe this is
                  the basis for escalating costs, not doctors'
                  fees. (p.57)

December 8	"CONFEREES ON AID TO AGED BACK 13% BENEFIT RISE." House of Representatives – Senate Conference Committee on Social Security agrees on rise in Medicare benefits while severe cuts in Medicaid are planned. (p.38)
December 13	"APPEAL ON MEDICAID IS SENT TO JOHNSON." Mayor Lindsay and Governor Rockefeller urge President Johnson to kill Social Security bill due to Medicaid restrictions. (p.39)
December 28	"PRESIDENT SIGNS D.C.'S CRIME BILL." President Johnson signs bill extending Medicare to 180,000 in Washington, D.C. (P.21)
December 30	"MEDICARE SUPPLEMENT WILL RISE IN COST TO $ 4.00." Health,Education,Welfare announces $ 1.00 increase to $ 4.00 in monthly premiums on voluntary insurance part of Medicare. (p.19)
January 15, 1968	"SENATE TO WIDEN INQUIRIES ON RISING HEALTH COSTS." Senate Committee plans hearings in 1968 on rising cost of health care; Labor Statistics Bureau studies indicate that hospital costs doubled and doctor fees rose 40% in past 10 years. (p.18)
March 5	"JOHNSON HEALTH PLAN ASKS STRESS ON DOCTOR TRAINING." President Johnson delivers special health message to Congress; Seeks to prevent unnecessary hospitalization and reduce cost by asking for authority to revise methods by which government calculates payment for hospital care and drugs. (p.1)
March 6	"MORE PHYSICIANS SOUGHT IN NATION." AMA President Rouse criticizes President Johnson's health message, urges government spending for health care to be moderated. (p.30)

March 24   "COHEN SUGGEST NEW WELFARE TAX."
                  Secretary-designate W.J. Cohen predicts
                  hospital costs will continue to rise but
                  doctor costs will taper off; Links Medicare
                  and Medicaid to higher costs. (p.51)

April 19   "JAVITS HESITATES ON LIBERAL OFFER."
                  Senator Javits charges administration has
                  cut back seriously on health care, sees
                  crisis. (p.51)

April 27   "DOCTORS GET PLEA TO SHUN FEE RISES."
                  Senate hearings in which Cohen urges
                  greater voluntary restraint by doctors in
                  fee rises; Ribicoff says major cost rise
                  came with onset of Medicare; Commissioner
                  Ball says Social Security Administration is
                  concerned. (p.40)

April 28   "SPIRALING MEDICAL COSTS REFLECT
                  DEFICIENCIES IN U.S. HEALTH CARE."
                  Survey of rising medical costs is charted.
                  (p.1)

June 19   "PANEL ADVANCES TAX RISE."
                  House of Representatives Rules Comm.
                  clears Administration tax rise. (p.1)

July 16   "HEALTH BENEFITS REPORTED ENHANCED
                  UNDER JOHNSON."
                  National Health Education Comm. report to
                  President Johnson shows health benefits
                  improved markedly since Johnson took
                  office. (p.10)

July 21   "STUDIES IN U.S. HEALTH."
                  Dr. Rusk comments on National Health
                  Education Comm. report. (p.59)

August 15   "PRESIDENT JOHNSON URGES
                  IMPROVEMENT OF MEDICARE."
                  President Johnson urges extension of
                  coverage for mothers and children from
                  prenatal through children's first year.
                  (p.30)

September 9   "MEDICAL CARE COSTS DOUBLES IN THREE
                  YEARS."
                  Tax Foundation report links big rise in
                  public outlay for health care to Medicare
                  and Medicaid. (p.47)

October 30	"PACE OF CONSUMER PRICE RISES WAS EASED DURING SEPTEMBER." Labor Statistics Bureau reports documented increase in medical costs over past twenty years. (p.20)
December 4	"BLUE CROSS ACTS ON RISING COSTS." Blue Cross sets program to stem rise in hospital costs by providing incentives to hospitals that improve efficiency. (p.21)
December 9	"GREAT SOCIETY: WHAT IT WAS, WHERE IT IS." New York Times survey of Johnson's achievement in health field is detailed. (p.41)
January 1, 1969	"MEDICARE PREMIUM LEFT AT $4.00 BY COHEN." Health, Education, and Welfare Secretary Cohen warns doctors to stop raising fees; concern over impact on Medicare. (p.1)
January 27	"U.S. HEALTH COSTS IN 1967 TOPPED $50-BILLING UP 12%." Health,Education,and Welfare Department report for 1967 health expenditures indicates that there has been a 12% increase in public and private expenditures for health. Rise linked to Medicare-Medicaid programs. (p.18)
March 28	"SENATE REPORT SAYS AGED SHOULD PAY MORE FOR MEDICARE." Senate Committee report states that aged must pay a greater share for Medicare." (p.21)
April 8	"U.S. FUND CUTS OFF IN THREE SCHOOL UNITS." Three Mississippi hospitals are denied further aid due to failure to comply with 1964 Civil Rights Act. (p.48)
July 11	"PRESIDENT WARNS OF 'MASSIVE CRISIS' IN HEALTH CARE." Secretary Finch (Health, Education, Welfare) issues report holding nation's resources are being overtaxed, used wastefully, and that inflation in health costs are grave. (p.1)

July 19   "KNOWLES CALLS FOR STEPS TO EASE MEDICAL BURDEN OF THE ELDERLY."
In testimony to Senate Subcommittee on Aged, Dr. Knowles urges action to ease fiscal burdens for elderly due to rising medical costs. (p.7)

August 6   "MEDICARE BRINGS DE BAKEY AND COOLEY $ 396,000."
Health, Education, Welfare reports that Medicare money is used for heart transplants. (p.78)

September 16   "RIBICOFF SEEKING A HEALTH POLICY."
Senator Ribicoff says he will propose the formation of a council of Health Advisors to help establish unified federal policy in the health area. (p.26)

October 29   "GARDNER URGES LOCALITIES TO REFORM HEALTH CARE."
Former Health, Education, Welfare Secretary Gardner urges coordination of all health care programs to establish principles of adequate health care for all Americans regardless of their ability to pay. (p.22)

November 15   "TEAR GAS ROUTS 2,000 IN CAPITAL CLASH."
2000 people protest across Health, Education, Welfare building asking Health, Education, Welfare to provide free medical care for all. (p.26)

December 20   "HEALTH CARE SYSTEM – A SICK BUT CURABLE SYSTEM."
Dr. L. Baumgartner discusses crisis in health care (U.S.) and prospects for remodeling system. (p.30)

January 1, 1970   "U.S. HEALTH UNITS FACE SLIM BUDGETS."
Health, Education, Welfare budget seen facing extremely tight money through mid–1971; Medicare budgets will get increase as there are no caps to them. (p.1)

January 12	"ADMINISTRATION SEEDS SHORT-RUN GAINS IN NATION'S MEDICAL SYSTEM." New York Times survey of Nixon Administration policy concludes that policy focuses on short-run gains rather than long-term issues. (p.19)
January 27	"PRESIDENT, ON T.V., VETOES SCHOOL AID AS INFLATIONARY." Nixon veto of $ 19.7 billion budget as inflationary. (p.1)
January 29	"NIXON SUSTAINED IN FUND BILL VETO BY LARGE MARGIN." House of Representatives upholds veto by 226-191 vote. (p.1)
February 25	"OVER HOSPITALIZING CHARGED BY DOCTOR." Senate Subcommittee blames unnecessary hospital admissions on insurance system and doctors who find hospitalization as more convenient. (p.56)
March 17	"U.S. HEALTH CALLED MUDDLED IN SENATE STUDY." Senator Ribicoff releases Subcommittee report stating that national health programs are cumbersome, disjointed, bureaucratic, etc. (p.1)
April 13	"EGEBERG FAVORS AID FOR ABORTION." Assistant Secretary of Health, Education, Welfare Egeberg says urgent health problem in U.S. is delivering system to insure all poor receive adequate care." (p.19)
May 5	"5% SOCIAL SECURITY BENEFIT RISE CLEARS WAYS AND MEANS PANEL." House of Representatives Committee passes bill to set standards for what the government will pay doctors under Social Security. (p.28)

97

May 26   "SOME OFFICIALS OF HEALTH, EDUCATION, WELFARE SAY HEALTH PART IS IN TROUBLE."
Article describes growing consensus among Health, Education, Welfare officials indicating that department's health services are in serious trouble; blame meddling by Nixon advisors. (p.20)

June 15   "FOR MICHAEL CRICHTON, MEDICINE IS FOR WRITING."
Article on M. Crichton, author, who blames AMA for spiraling costs – the major problem facing medicine. (p.48)

August 23   "U.S. CHAMBER SEEKS A HEALTH CARE PLAN."
U.S. Chamber of Commerce establishes 16 member group of executives to develop plan for better health care in response to growing concern with health costs by business and industry. (p.52)

September 27   "HEALTH SPENDING IS TRIPLED BY U.S."
AMA study of federal budget shows government expenditures have tripled in annual spending for medicine and health in last 5 years. (p.38)

October 16   "PRESIDENT MEETING DELAY ON HIS DOMESTIC REFORM."
Summary of Nixon's proposals and congressional actions concerning health care in its 20 months is presented. (p.22)

November 24   "A HOSPITAL PANEL ASKS HEALTH PLAN."
American Hospital Association recommends establishment of AMERI-PLAN, which if implemented, is supposedly able to do away with Medicaid and Medicare. (p.28)

"CHIROPRACTOR SERVICE VOTED."
Senate Finance Committee votes to add chiropractor service, as a covered service, to Medicare at a projected cost of $ 75 million. (p.44)

January 18, 1971   "SENATE PANEL ON AGING, AFTER 2 YEAR STUDY, SAYS RETIREMENT INCOME HAS REACHED CRISIS STAGE."
Senate Committee on Aging Report reveals that the health bill for the elderly (over 65) is 6 times as much as for youth and 2 1/2 times as much as for people in 16 – 64 group; Medicare is found to pay less than half of cost. (p.11)

January 26   "23 SENATORS SUPPORT NEW PLAN FOR NATIONAL HEALTH INSURANCE."
A bill is to be introduced in House of Representatives covering drugs for Medicare beneficiaries; estimated cost $ 1 billion per year. (p.20)

February 3   "PRESIDENT TO ASK MEDICARE FEE RISE AND BENEFIT CUTS."
Nixon Administration health care proposals to include cut in Medicare hospital benefits and use in payments by 20 million citizens covered by program. (p.1)

February 14   "NO CURE YET FOR RISING BILL."
Problems facing Nixon Administration in curbing spiraling Medicare costs are outlined. Section D. (p.8)

February 16   "BUILDING UNIONS EXPECT FREEZE ON PAY AND PRICES."
AFL–CIO President Meany states that the first legislative priority of labor is the passage of a National Health Plan. (p.49)

February 19   "NIXON'S PROGRAM ON HEALTH CARE PROPOSES THAT EMPLOYERS PAY $ 2,5 BILLION MORE A YEAR."
Nixon unveils proposals for improving health care by tapping private rather than public section; provisions of Medicare changes are outlined. (p.17)

March 18   "BILL WOULD LIST DOCTORS."
Senator Andersen introduces bill requiring a public listing of doctors receiving $10,000 or more from Medicare." (p.32)

March 19	"9.6% RATE RISE WON BY JERSEY BLUE CROSS." New Jersey Insurance Department grants Blue Cross an average 9.6% increase, but Medicare beneficiaries with insurance that complements Medicare are exempt." (p.43)
April 2	"STATES MAY GAIN IN WELFARE PLAN." House Ways and Means Committee is considering legislation that would require Medicare beneficiaries to pay 1/8 of hospital costs beginning with 15th day. (p.43)
April 3	"HOUSE UNIT SPLIT ON MEDICARE COSTS." Nixon proposals for cost containment of Medicare programs are presented. (p.30)
April 4	"BROADER MEDICARE URGED BY U.S. ADVISORY COUNCIL." Federal Advisory Council proposes expansion of Medicare to cover partial payment of prescription drugs for non-hospitalized elderly with financing by employers, employees, and federal government. (p.1)
April 5	"SENATE PANEL SAYS FEDERAL PROGRAMS FAIL TO MEET NEEDS OF ELDERLY." Senate Committee on Aging urges financing of Medicare through payroll taxes with no charges for elderly. (p.24)
May 13	"PANEL INCREASES HEALTH BENEFITS." House of Representatives Ways and Means Committee refuses to accept Nixon proposals to reduce Medicare benefits by over $800 million; agrees to extend program to 1.5 million disabled under age 65; retain benefits at current level. (p.40)
June 23	"HOUSE APPROVES WELFARE REFORM BY 288-132 VOTE." House of Representatives approves Omnibus bill including major changes in Medicare; changes are outlined. (p.1)

August 6   "HEALTH COST RISE OF 50% PREDICTED."
Social Security Administration study of national health insurance proposals concludes that all of them would result in significant increases in medical costs. (p.91)

August 9   "AMERICANS NOW FAVOR A NATIONAL HEALTH PLAN."
A New York Times survey shows growing support for National Health Insurance as people are frustrated with higher taxes for government programs and failure of private insurance to curb costs and the inability of many Americans to secure the health care they want. (p.1)

October 2   "HOSPITAL PATIENTS' COST TO RISE UNDER MEDICARE BY $ 8.00 TO $68.00."
Health, Education, Welfare Secretary Richardson announces fee increase effective 1/1/72. (p.1)

October 20   "MILLS AND RICHARDSON DISAGREE AS MEDICARE HEARING OPEN."
Long-awaited hearings on national health insurance are initiated by Rep. Mills' Committee. (p.28)

January 1, 1972   "MEDICARE FEES TO RISE BY 20 CENTS NEXT JULY."
Secretary Richardson announces increased rate of $ 5.80 monthly, effective 7/1, for medical insurance rate of Medicare; an increase of 20 cents per month. (p.6)

January 17   "LIBERAL DEMOCRATS PRESS FOR HEALTH INSURANCE PLANK ON PLATFORM."
Democratic Policy Council Planning Committee hopes to adopt comprehensive natural health insurance as party plank. (p.16)

January 18   "KENNEDY SAYS PRESIDENT HAS FAILED TO CARRY OUT 'PROMISE OF AMERICA'."
Senator Kennedy calls for a program of National Health Insurance to provide health care for all citizens. (p.17)

January 21	"CONGRESS SEEMS RESPONSIVE TO NIXON'S APPEAL TO ENACT HIS LEGISLATION PROGRAM." President Nixon introduces legislation to create National Health Insurance program in State of the Union Message. (p.19)
January 21	"NIXON BIDS CONGRESS DROP MEDICARE COVERAGE CHARGE." President Nixon renews his recommendation that Congress eliminate charges to elderly for doctor's fees under Medicare, saving beneficiaries estimated $ 1.5 billion per year. (p.19)
January 25	"HEALTH CARE FUND WILL INCREASE BUT RISE IN FEES SHOULD SLOW." Government report indicates that Medicare costs will continue to rise in 1972 to $10 billion, an increase of $ 1.5 billion. (p.18)
February 11	"HEALTH CARE PLAN WIDENED BY HEALTH, EDUCATION, WELFARE." Nixon Administration proposes legislation in form of amendments to pending NHI Partnership Act. Employers will be mandated to offer private health insurance to workers and families. Federal subsidization of near-poor and bad risks still unresolved. Seen as victory for Secretary Richardson. (p.1)
February 19	"TWO INSURERS CITE EARNINGS GAIN." Insurance executive says that issue of NHI may become 1972 Presidential campaign issue. (p.48)
February 22	"HEALTH LEGISLATION: A PROGRESS REPORT." Review article compares NHI proposals made by Kennedy, Long, and Nixon. (p.53)
February 29	"McCARTHY URGES PROGRAM ON NATIONAL HEALTH CARE." Ex-Senator McCarthy, campaigning in Illinois, urges nationally subsidized health insurance program. (p.22)

March 2   "JACKSON, IN FLORIDA, CALLS FOR SOCIAL
           SECURITY RISE."
           Senator Jackson, campaigning in Florida,
           would correct for Medicare's weakness by
           adding drugs, laboratory tests, eyeglasses,
           and dental work. (p.28)

March 4   "MILLS PROPOSES OWN HEALTH PLAN."
           Congressman Mills, Presidential aspirant,
           outlines his plan for NHI. (p.19)

March 8   "U.S. AUDITORS ACCUSE INSURERS OF
           COSTLY MISTAKES IN MEDICARE."
           Medicare audits reveal insurance companies
           fail   to   limit   doctor's   payments   to
           "reasonable, customary and usual" fees
           standards. (p.19)

March 29   "HUMPHREY SAYS NIXON IGNORES NEEDS
           OF AGED."
           Senator Humphrey criticizes President
           Nixon for ignoring recommendations of
           1971 White House Conference on Aging to
           liberalize Medicare benefits. (p.24)

May 24   "INSURERS HOLD ANNUAL MEETING."
           National Liberty Corporation reports best
           year in selling health insurance especially
           Medicare supplement. (p.62)

June 10   "RISE OF 10% VOTED IN SOCIAL SECURITY."
           Senator Long decides not to pursue
           coverage for catastrophic illnesses, which
           would have cost $ 3.3 billion yearly.
           (p.14)

June 14   "MAJOR PROVISIONS OF SENATE BILL ON
           SOCIAL SECURITY AND WELFARE."
           Senate Finance Committee tentatively
           approves Social Security bill that calls for
           extending Medicare to such services as
           chiropractic and prescription drugs. (p.32)

June 18   "KENNEDY AND MILLS URGE HEALTH PLAN
           FOR 1972 PLATFORM."
           Senator Kennedy and Rep. Mills make
           public text of proposals urging Democratic
           Party to adopt compulsory national health
           insurance as platform plank. (p.23)

June 22   "NEW AMA CHIEF HITS HEALTH PLAN."
AMA President opposes national health insurance on the grounds that its costs and abuse would be tremendous. (p.23)

July 9   "LAG IN MEDICARE HARD TO HOSPITALS."
New York State Controller Levitt reprots New York City Hospital system suffers from an average delay in payment of 229 days amounting to $ 9.2 million. (p.28)

"JERSEY CUTS HEALTH COSTS BY STRESSING HOME CARE."
New Jersey Health Association says Medicare was saved $ 3.5 million because of its emphasis on home and nursing home care. (p.61)

July 25   "TWO G.O.P. POLLS RATE BUSING ISSUE LOW."
Republican party opinion poll indicates that 47% favor national health insurance whereas 44% oppose. (p.18)

July 31   "WINDFALL TO HELP CITY'S HOSPITALS."
Increase in Medicare and Medicaid payments (43%) since 1970 has allowed New York City to end its personnel attrition policy. (p.36)

August 13   "HOSPITALS LEAVING MEDICARE PROGRAM."
GAO report finds that 5,000 hospitals and nursing homes withdraw from Medicare program due to red tape and bookkeeping problems. (p.87)

August 22   "PLATFORM SEEMS CERTAIN OF APPROVAL."
Republican and Democratic party platforms take opposite stands re: NHI. (p.36)

September 21   "McGOVERN CALLS FOR MORE AID TO AGED."
Senator McGovern, Democratic Presidential candidate, favors immediate expansion of Medicare to cover out-of-hospital prescription costs. (p.40)

104

September 28   "KENNEDY ASSURES DOCTORS ON PLAN."
                American Academy of Family Physicians
                supports Medicredit, plan supported by
                AMA, which calls for tax credits for
                purchase of health insurance. Medicredit
                is viewed as alternative to National Health
                Insurance. (p.21)
September 30   "SENATE VOTE BARS CUT IN WELFARE AS
                PENSION RISE."
                Senate votes to extend Medicare coverage
                to hearing aids, eye care, glasses, foot
                care and dental care. (p.1)
October 3   "SOCIAL SECURITY RISE BECOMES A
                NIGHTMARE FOR MANY ELDERLY."
                New York Times survey of impact of
                recent 20% increase in Social Security
                reveals that many recipients are now
                ineligible for Medicaid, which leaves them
                without medical insurance. (p.1)
October 4   "ROCKEFELLER BIDS CONGRESS ACT ON
                WELFARE AND MEDICAID."
                Governor Rockefeller calls on Congress to
                pass legislation to prevent the 93,000
                recipients being declared ineligible to
                Medicaid due to rise in Medicare. (p.22)
October 6   "WIDE BILL ON WELFARE AND SOCIAL
                SECURITY PASSES SENATE 68-5."
                Senate passes most costly Social Security
                bill including provision preventing loss of
                insurance coverage as identified in New
                York Times survey. (p.1)
October 8   "INCREASE IN DEDUCTIBLE COST OF
                MEDICARE IS CUT IN HALF."
                Deductible for Medicare in 1973 to rise
                from $ 68 to $ 72. (p.42)
October 15   "CONGRESS SHELVES WELFARE REFORM."
                Senate and House of Representatives
                conferees agree on compromise legislation;
                extend coverage to disabled under 65 but
                eliminates payment of prescriptions. (p.39)

October 22   "NIXON IS REPORTED CONSIDERING A VETO OF HUGE MEDICAL AND PENSION BENEFITS BILL."
                President Nixon considering veto of compromised legislation that passed both houses. (p.69)

October 31   "NIXON SIGNS $5 BILLION BILL EXPANDING SOCIAL SECURITY."
                President Nixon signs into law $ 5 billion Social Security bill that will expand Medicare coverage to include people under 65 for first time including disabled and those suffering from acute kidney disease. (p.1)

November 11   "RATE OF INFLATION CONTINUES HIGHER THAN NIXON GOAL."
                Rise in health insurance premiums given as basis for October rise in consumer prices. (p.1)

December 24   "PENSION BENEFITS AND COSTS TO RISE."
                First 1973 paychecks for U.S. workers will outline changes in Social Security benefits and costs. (p.28)

January 4, 1973 "MEDICARE COST UP 50 CENTS A MONTH ON JULY 1."
                Social Security Administration announces increases in charges for Medicare recipients, 3rd raise to become effective in 1973.   Increases attributed to higher hospital charges and doctors' fees. (p.34)

January 5   "$ 1 BILLION ASKED FOR 20 CITY HOSPITALS."
                Two-thirds of New York City Health and Hospital Corporation $ 1 billion+ annual budget comes from Medicare, Medicaid, and Blue Cross. (p.35)

January 14   "AUDIT ASSAILS CITY ON MEDICARE BILLS."
                New York State Controller Levitt charges New York City Hospital system with failure to bill for "substantial amounts" of money due it for services provided Medicare patients on an ambulatory basis. (p.47)

106

January 14   "MEDICARE LESSONS."
                    New York Times editorial raising questions
                    about ability of congressmen to understand
                    economic impact of extending Medicare
                    benefits. Section D. (p.16)
January 30   "NIXON URGES PUBLIC TO SEEK BUDGET
                    LID."
                    Nixon Administration plans to seek
                    legislation that will require elderly to pay
                    sharply increased share of their hospital
                    costs; action to trigger opposition form
                    senior citizen groups. (p.1)
January 31   "TWO DEMOCRATS SEE CURB ON
                    MEDICARE."
                    Senator Kennedy and Rep. Griffith call
                    Nixon plans for increases in Medicare fees
                    to be hostile acts. (p.19)
February 1   "CONCERN ACCUSED OF MEDICARE
                    FRAUD."
                    Court suit brought against G & D Surgical
                    Drug Co. for alleged filing of false claims
                    for $ 13,479. (p.75)
March 2   "CONGRESS ACTS TO RESTORE RURAL AID."
                    Senate Democrats attack President Nixon's
                    proposal to have elderly pay larger share
                    of hospital and doctor costs under
                    Medicare. (p.14)
March 6   "PLAN TO CUT AGED'S MEDICARE
                    ASSAILED."
                    A. Brophy, director of New Your City
                    Office of Aging assails Nixon Proposal.
                    Proposed changes will offset recent 20%
                    increase in Social Security. (p.30)
March 19   "MEDICARE REPORT TO BE MADE PUBLIC."
                    Social Security Administration says it will
                    make public all future Medicare Survey
                    and investigation reports. Earlier reports
                    will remain confidential. (p.27)
March 25   "MONDALE URGING MEDICARE STAND."
                    Senator Mondale and 50 U.S. Senators
                    introduce legislation barring Nixon-
                    proposed fee changes from going into
                    effect; e.g., 60-day hospitalization in Nixon
                    plan would cost a minimum of $500
                    whereas, it is now $72. (p.50)

April 8   "WOODCOCK SCORES AMA HEALTH PLAN."
United Auto Workers President L.
Woodcock says labor-backed national
health insurance plan is preferable to AMA
proposal. (p.80)

April 12   "BUSINESS PANEL PRESENTS HEALTH PLAN."
Committee for Economic Development, a
business-oriented group, releases proposal
that incorporates the premise of universal
change. Estimated cost in first year would
be $5 billion more than presently spent.
(p.20)

May 6   "MEDICARE RESOLUTION VOTED."
International Longshoremen's and
Warehouse's Union adopted resolution
asking that costs for Medicare be paid
from federal income tax rather than
payroll tax system. (p.84)

May 17   "GROUP HEALTH PLAN PASSED BY SENATE."
U.S. Senate, 69-25, passes $805 million bill
authorizing federal funds to encourage
group health plans that will be provided
funds to enroll the poor. (p.51)

June 10   "NEEDS OF THE ELDERLY IN SUFFOLK
STUDIED."
A study of elderly in Suffolk County, New
York State, found that Medicare and
Medicaid are relatively effective in
servicing needs of the aged. (p.112)

June 13   "U.S. COURT UPSETS BAN ON MEDICARE
TO ALIEN REFUGEES."
U.S. District Court judge ruled that
Medicare cannot be denied to aliens who
pay payroll taxes. (p.44)

June 25   "THIRD OF AMA DOCTORS POLLED WOULD
BOYCOTT NATIONAL SYSTEM."
AMA releases survey of doctors indicating
that one-third of them would boycott
National Health Insurance plan as proposed
by Kennedy-Griffith. (p.10)

June 28   "BLUE SHIELD SEEKS 36.9% RISE IN RATES FOR PUBLIC EMPLOYEES."
New York City Labor Commissioner Gotbaum is investigating rates charged by Electronic Data Systems for computerizing Medicare billing systems as too high. Electronic Data Systems is owned by R. Perot. (p.59)

July 6   "RISE IN MEDICARE DEDUCTION TO BE ROLLED BACK IN FREEZE."
President Nixon freezes for 60 days increases in Medicare fees. (p.20)

July 7   "SECOND-CLASS MEDICARE."
Letter to editor charges Medicare discriminates against rural areas by setting fee schedules that are almost one-half of urban areas. (p.20)

October 10   "WEINBERGER DROPS SUGGESTION TO END MEDICAL DEDUCTIONS."
Health, Education, Welfare Director Weinberger expects Congress will not take any action on administration's National Health Insurance Plan. (p.13)

November 19   "MEDICARE HELD 'GOLD MINE' FOR DOCTORS IN MANHATTAN."
Federal government, in first public disclosure of Medicare fees charged by doctors, reveals Manhattan-based doctors usually charge more for identical services that other New York City doctors. Blue Shield executive C.F. Amiratz states that Medicare has been a "gold mine" for doctors. (p.1)

November 25   "MEDICARE FEES AREN'T HURTING HIS HEALTH."
Follow-up story comparing differential charges made by doctors. Section D. (p.4)

November 29   "SENATE BACKS MORE FOR MEDICARE DRUGS."
U.S. Senate, 77-11, adds amendment to allow elderly to obtain drugs on a non-hospitalized basis. Expected to cost additional $700 million per year. Social Security taxes to increase to 5.9% for both employers and employees. (p.56)

| December 12 | "SOCIAL ILLS CALLED KEY TO HEALTH CARE." |

December 12   "SOCIAL ILLS CALLED KEY TO HEALTH CARE."
Blue Cross president W.J. McNearney says NHI will not alter basic illness pattern as education and housing are significant factors in etiology. (p.64)

December 23   "SEEKING A BETTER WAY IN MEDICARE."
Review of legislation passed by Congress to establish HMO. Section D. (p.8)

December 25   "ACTION BY 93rd CONGRESS."
Summary of Nixon's proposals and action concerning health care. (p.14)

December 30   "PRESIDENT SIGNS BILL FOR REFORM IN MEDICAL CARE."
President Nixon signs into law HMO Act of 1973; should help shift emphasis of medical care to prevention from treatment; $50 million set aside to see projects actually work. (p.1)

January 4, 1974   "PRESIDENT SIGNS 11% PENSION RISE."
6.4% increase to $6.70 per month on optimal Medicare insurance premium effective July 1st is approved. (p.34)

January 9   "PRESIDENT TO ASK WIDE HEALTH PLAN."
President Nixon expected to propose to Congress in January a national health insurance program for all Americans. (p.1)

January 10   "HOPES FOR NATIONAL HEALTH PLAN RISE."
Nixon national health insurance will vie with other plans already presented to Congress. (p.27)

January 13   "HEALTH INSURANCE FOR EVERYONE."
Nixon's plan reviewed; covers all Americans and relies primarily on contributions by employers. Section D. (p.2)

February 2   "INSURING HEALTH."
New York Times editorial lauds Nixon plan's scope but criticizes its reliance on private insurance system – too bureaucratic. (p.28)

February 6   "NIXON SEES PASSAGE IN 1974 OF A HEALTH INSURANCE PLAN."
Nixon predicts some form of comprehensive national health insurance will be enacted in 1974. (p.16)

February 7   "NIXON OFFERS HEALTH INSURANCE PROGRAM WITH COSTS PUT AT $5.9 BILLION A YEAR."
Nixon's national health insurance plan presented to Congress. No new taxes and dependent on insurance industry. Kennedy criticizes latter. (p.34)

February 8   "DESPITE BROAD COVERAGE OF NIXON'S NEW HEALTH INSURANCE PLAN, CRITICS SAY IT HAS SERIOUS FLAWS."
Analysis of Nixon plan with comments from variety of sources. (p.12)

February 9   "U.S. DROPS HOSPITAL REVIEW PLAN THAT WAS OPPOSED BY DOCTORS."
Health, Education, Welfare abandons idea to review hospitalization decision of doctors so that only necessary hospitalizations would occur. AMA threatens legal suit as plan was infringement on doctors' right to hospitalize their patients. (p.58)

February 16   "UNHEALTHY RHETORIC."
New York Times editorial says Nixon plan fails to correct for maldistribution of health personnel and lack of preventive health care. Urges negotiations with Congressional leaders. (p.30)

February 27   "NIXON DECLARES DEMOCRATIC LAG."
Secretary Weinberger reports that President Nixon is distressed that no hearings have been scheduled on his national health insurance plan. (p.18)

March 18   "MEDICARE'S POLICY ON FEES CRITICIZED."
Rep. Elizabeth Holtzman charges that Medicare reimbursement to the elderly averages 60% rather than standard of 80%, costing the elderly $70 million in 1973. (p.62)

April 3	"MILLS, KENNEDY BACK HEALTH PLAN SIMILAR TO NIXON." Senator Kennedy and Rep. Mills introduce new national health insurance plan; enhances likelihood of passage. (p.1)
April 7	"HEALTH PLAN PROGRESS." New York Times editorial praises Kennedy and Mills plan as sensible compromise between early Kennedy plan and Nixon plan. Section D. (p.16)
April 18	"WEINBERGER SEES A SHARP RISE IN HOSPITAL COSTS." New rules for kidney disease announced by Health, Education, Welfare to reduce current Medicare costs of $250 million for 13,000 patients. (p.45)
April 25	"PANEL QUESTIONS WEINBERGER ON NIXON'S HEALTH PLAN." Hearings on Nixon's National Health Insurance plan held before House Ways and Means Committee with Congressman Mills presiding. Mills criticizes plan. (p.28)
April 28	"CONTROLS ENDING WITH U.S. IN GRIP OF STEEP INFLATION." New York Times survey reveals that hospital fees have soared in large part because Medicare has intensified demand for health services. (p.42)
May 14	"SUMMARY OF VARIOUS ACTIONS TAKEN BY THE U.S. SUPREME COURT." U.S. Supreme court agrees to hear appeal as to whether Cuban refugees qualify for Medicare. (p.18)
May 21	"PRESIDENT EASES HEALTH-AID STAND." President Nixon makes radio address urging passage of his national health insurance plan with some compromises. (p.1) "PROTECTION AGAINST ILLNESS." New York Times editorial praises President Nixon for willingness to compromise on National Health Insurance plan. (p.40)

May 28   "CONGRESS LAGS ON HEALTH INSURANCE DESPITE ACCORD ON NEED FOR ACTION," Senate Finance Committee and House Ways and Means Committee cannot agree on National Health Insurance; stumbling blocks are how payments are to be made by employers and employees and how much additional government funds should be used. (p.52)

June 13   "RAND REPORT PREDICTS ANY NATIONAL HEALTH INSURANCE PLAN WOULD SWAMP DOCTORS' OFFICES AND CLINICS." Rand Corporation report says any National Health Insurance plan will deluge doctors' offices and out-patient clinics but have little effect on hospitalization rates. (p.31)

July 11   "HEALTH PLAN'S COST PUT AT $6,5 BILLION." Cost estimates of various National Health Insurance plans analyzed by Nixon administration. (p.18)

July 21   "AGREED: HERE COMES NATIONAL HEALTH INSURANCE; QUESTION: WHAT KIND?" Article by Alice Rivlin outlining why National Health Insurance is needed; inadequate coverage for poor and fails to protect against catastrophic illness, biased to high cost care and discourages preventative medicine. Section F. (p.8)

July 26   "BEAME SIGNS BILL ON LISTING OF CIVIL SERVICE JOB NEWS." New York City increases reimbursement of individual Medicare Part B from $6.00 to $6.70 per month. (p.30)

August 13   "TRANSCRIPT OF PRESIDENT FORD'S ADDRESS TO JOINT SESSION OF CONGRESS AND THE NATION." President Ford urges passage of National Health Insurance in speech to Congress. (p.20)

August 21   "HOUSE UNIT CLEARS A HEALTH-BILL PLAN."
House Ways and Means Committee, by a 12 to 11 vote, tentatively approves of key financing features of National Health Insurance Plan. (p.19)

August 22   "HOUSE PANEL RIFT APPEARS TO DOOM HEALTH COST BILL."
Rep. Mills adjourns meeting focusing on National Health Insurance compromise on the grounds of a lack of majority consensus. (p.1)

August 23   "WALKOUT ON HEALTH."
New York Times editorial criticizes Rep. Mills saying alternative is all or nothing approach, which won't be enacted. (p.28)

August 27   "U.S. HEALTH INSURANCE: A LEGISLATIVE GOAL THAT HAS NO FOES STALLED BY DIFFERENCES IN APPROACH."
Analyses of Congressional action in regard to National Health Insurance including role played by Congressman Mills; miscalculation of latent conflicts among committee members. (p.20)

September 13   "FORD PRESENTS CONGRESS WITH PRIORITY LIST FOR ACTION."
President Ford includes National Health Insurance as part of priority list of action by Congress. (p.18)

September 16   "MR. FORD'S PRIORITIES."
New York Times editorial criticizes Ford's gentle support for National Health Insurance. (p.34)

October 6   "MEDICARE RAISING COST TO PATIENTS."
Secretary Weinberger announces increase in deductible for 23.5 million Medicare beneficiaries from $84 to $92 beginning 1/1/75. (p.64)

October 6   "RIBICOFF SEEKS A FREEZE."
Senator Ribicoff introduces legislation freezing Medicare deductible at $84. (p.64)

October 24   "GOVERNMENT IS MAILING NEW MEDICARE BOOKLET."

New Medicare booklet is being mailed to the 23.5 million beneficiaries; first update since 1968. (p.43)

November 29   "HEALTH, EDUCATION, WELFARE SETS POLICY TO POLICE DOCTORS."

Health, Education, Welfare announces utilization review program to monitor doctors' and hospitals' practices in regard to Medicare and Medicaid. (p.19)

December 24   "$25 BILLION, 5 YEAR HEALTH PLAN DOWN PLAYS NATIONAL HEALTH INSURANCE."

Health, Education, Welfare report states that safer working conditions and special medical projects rather than National Health Insurance are key to improved health in America. (p.42)

December 26   "SENATE STUDY FINDS A DROP IN MEDICARE HURTS THE ELDERLY."

Report released by Senate Special Committee on Aging states that 11.2 million elderly spend $500 million on additional insurance per year due to all the gaps in existing program. (p.30)

January 20, 1975 "SOCIAL SECURITY UNIT SHIFTS ON MEDICARE."

Social Security Advisory Council reverses itself and votes, 9-4, to recommend financing Medicare hospital benefits out of general revenues rather increase payroll taxes for those earning upper incomes in 1976. (p.18)

January 25   "SOCIAL SECURITY BENEFITS TO TOP RECEIPTS IN 1976, PANEL REPORTS."

Social Security Advisory Council holds news conference in which proposals to alter financing of Medicare to one-half from general revenues and one-half Social Security payroll tax are outlines. New method of financing should meet the problem of large deficits being experienced by Medicare. (p.1)

February 4	"MOST SOCIAL WELFARE PROGRAMS WILL BE HARD HIT BY CUTBACKS." Review article indicating that Ford administration will ask Medicare recipients to pay large share of costs of hospital treatment and physicians services. (p.21)
February 21	"AMA SUING U.S. OVER PEER REVIEW." AMA files suit in effort to block implementation of Health, Education, Welfare regulations that would set up system of medical peer review to evaluate physician's decision to hospitalize Medicare and Medicaid patients within day of admission. (p.1)
March 8	"FORD REJECTS PLAN TO PAY MEDICARE OUT OF TREASURY." President Ford rejects the recommendation of Social Security Advisory Council to solve impending financial problems of Medicare by shifting some of the financing to general tax revenues. (p.28)
April 6	"FORD DEFICIT GOAL CALLED UNLIKELY." President Ford proposes a $12 billion package of spending reductions in Medicare to hold budget deficit at $60 million. Patients to pay larger share of hospital bill. (p.22)
April 10	"PERSONAL FINANCE: OTHER INSURANCE IS HELPFUL IN FILLING MEDICARE GAP." Review article describing gap between Medicare bill and payment leading half of beneficiaries to subscribe to private supplementary plans. (p.64)
April 14	"PERSONAL FINANCE: AUGMENTING MEDICARE." Second review article regarding supplementary insurance plans for Medicare is outlined. (p.51)
April 17	"1,151 COUNT COMPLAINT FILED AGAINST DOCTOR FOR FRAUD." Federal government files 1,151-count civil complaint against Dr. Pablo K. Chan, charging him with Medicare fraud and asking for $2.3 million in charges. (p.27)

April 29	"HEMPSTEAD CENTER FOR HEALTH SERVICES ACCUSED OF ABUSES." New York State Welfare Inspector General office's investigation discloses abuses in health care provided Medicaid and Medicare patients at Hempstead Medical Services. (p.37)
May 4	"HEALTH, EDUCATION, WELFARE CALLED NEGLECTFUL IN CHECKING RELIEF FRAUD." Congressional investigations charge that Health, Education, Welfare is guilty of neglect as there are only 13 criminal investigations to police Medicare programs. (p.55)
May 10	"COURT BACKS REVIEW OF U.S. HEALTH BILLS." Professional Standards Review Act of 1972 was ruled constitutional by 3 judge Federal panel. Act allows organizations to review bills submitted for Medicare payment. Suit brought by Association of American Physicians and Surgeons. (p.21)
May 17	"ABUSES IN MEDICARE PUT AT $27 MILLION IN LAST FIVE YEARS." Abuse and fraud have led Social Security Administration to report that it was overcharged in the Medicare program by $27 million. (p.25)
May 28	"JUDGE BARS REVIEW BOARDS AT HOSPITALS." A federal district judge grants preliminary injunction, requested by AMA, to bar Health, Education, Welfare from implementing regulations requiring evaluations of doctor's decision to hospitalize Medicare patients. (p.24)
May 31	"AMA LIBERALIZES TO DRAW YOUNG DOCTORS." AMA, faced with declining membership and growing financial deficits, is liberalizing its image and cooperating with Health, Education, Welfare in establishing Medicare peer review. (p.55)

June 3   "SUIT IS FILED TO VOID MEDICARE RULES."
          American Medical College Association has filed suit against Health, Education, Welfare in attempt to declare new regulations (limits on charges) as invalid. (p.20)

July 2   "BACKLOG IS EASED ON NURSING HOMES."
          Social Security Administration releases backlog of costs reports provided by providers of Medicare but remains silent as to why over payment claims dating from 1967 have remained unresolved. (p.30)

July 9   "INVESTORS TURNING TO HOSPITAL BONDS."
          Hospital tax-exempt bonds, possible since passage of Medicare in 1966, are growing in popularity. (p.52)

July 30   "MEDICARE AND MEDICAID AFTER DECADE: MIXED PICTURE OF GAINS AND EXCESSES."
          10th anniversary of signing of Medicare results in report being released indicating that program results are mixed. (p.12)

August 10 "HOSPITAL LOSES ON MEDICARE."
          U.S. Appeals Court, 5th Circuit, rules that Health, Education, Welfare has legal rights to recover monies charged for unnecessary medical services to Medicare. (p.22)

August 26 "BLUE CROSS ASKS INCREASE OF 23% IN RATE FOR 1976."
          Blue Cross and Blue Shield of Greater New York asks for rate increase for Medicare supplementary insurance policies. (p.1)

August 31 "STATE INVESTIGATING 4TH HEALTH FACILITY."
          New York Attorney General (Louis Lefkowitz) announces investigation of possible Medicare fraud cases. (p.82)

September 5   "HEALTH, EDUCATION, WELFARE
                   WITHDRAWS RULES ON HOSPITALS: AMA
                   DROPS SUIT."
                   Health, Education, Welfare withdraws new
                   regulations that would require hospitals to
                   police Medicare and Medicaid patients.
                   AMA drops legal suit. Cost issue a factor
                   in proposed regulations.   (p.10)

October 1   "MEDICARE PATIENTS TO PAY 13% MORE
                   FOR HOSPITALIZATION."
                   Medicare rates for hospital reimbursement
                   to increase 13% on 1/1/76.   (p.91)

October 28   "BYRNE ASSAILS U.S. ON MEDICARE CUTS."
                   Governor Byrne of New Jersey says
                   proposed federal Medicare cuts will cost
                   New Jersey residents at least $37 million.
                   (p.72)

November 18   "DOCTORS LOSE PLEA OVER MONITORING."
                   U.S. Supreme court rules without comment,
                   that lower federal district decision re:
                   constitutionality of peer review is correct.
                   (p.1)

November 26   "HEALTH SPENDING $118 BILLION A YEAR."
                   Social Security Administration Report
                   indicates Medicare costs rose 30% in one
                   year.   (p.37)

December 23   "JERSEY BLUE CROSS ASKS RATE
                   INCREASE."
                   Blue Cross – Blue Cross of New Jersey is
                   asking for rate increase in supplementary
                   insurance to match increases in hospital
                   reimbursement, which become effective
                   1/1/76.   (p.53)

January 12, 1976   "HEALTH, EDUCATION, WELFARE ESCAPING
                   FORD'S BUDGET CUTTING WITH HELP OF
                   CONGRESS AND BECAUSE OF INFLATED
                   COSTS."
                   Medicare and Medicaid rose 30% and 25%
                   respectively in fiscal 1975.   (p.12)

January 17   "PRESIDENT TO PROPOSE RISE IN THE
                   SOCIAL SECURITY TAX."
                   President Ford will propose increased costs
                   and benefits under Medicare in State of
                   Union Message.   (p.1)

January 20   "TRANSCRIPT OF PRESIDENT'S STATE OF THE UNION MESSAGE TO JOINT SESSION OF CONGRESS."
President Ford proposes catastrophic health insurance rather than National Health Insurance. (p.18)

January 22   "LIMITING THE COST OF MAJOR ILLNESS WOULD BENEFIT 3 MILLION PATIENTS."
President Ford proposes to limit elderly payment to $500 per year for hospitalization costs under Medicare; criticisms noted. (p.25)

January 23   "JACKSON PUSHES HEALTH PROGRAM."
Senator Henry Jackson calls for National Health Insurance and extension of Medicare benefits. (p.25)

January 24   "FORD TERMED LOW ON MEDICARE COST."
Informed sources state that President Ford erred in his estimation of cost to pay for catastrophic illness; actual cost will double $538 million as stated by President. (p.21)

January 29   "U.S. HAS LITTLE INFLUENCE ON HOW DOCTORS PRACTICE."
Professional Standards Review Organizations, established by Medicare in 1972, has not had regulations passed indicating how they should function. (p.24)

February 2   "MEDICARE WASTES MILLIONS BY RENTING MEDICAL AIDS."
Audits of Medicare records in New York City reveal loophole abuses resulting in rental charges for equipment exceeding purchase costs by 600%. (p.1)

February 9   "MANSFIELD AND SCOTT BACK CATASTROPHIC HEALTH PROJECT."
Senators Mansfield and Scott endorse catastrophic health insurance for all Americans, not just Medicare recipients. (p.21)

120

February 10   "FORD SENDS CONGRESS PLAN ON
                PENSIONS AND MEDICARE."
                Ford's proposal for Catastrophic Health
                Insurance sent to Congress; criticized by
                National Council for Senior Citizens.
                (p.30)

March 24   "HOUSE BUDGET CHIEF URGES $18.6
                BILLION MORE OUTLAY THAN FORD."
                Congressman Adams, House of
                Representatives Budget Committee
                Chairman, says revision of Medicare will
                result in $890 million savings. (p.68)

March 25   "CURBS SOUGHT FOR MEDICARE-
                MEDICAID COSTS, BUT NOT THE
                BENEFITS."
                Senator Talmadge hopes to curb Medicare
                expenditures by restricting administrative
                and payment systems while benefits and
                eligibility will remain untouched. (p.51)

April 17   "CARTER PROPOSES U.S. HEALTH PLAN."
                Presidential hopeful Jimmy Carter favors
                National Health Insurance to be financed
                by payroll taxes and general revenues.
                (p.1)

May 7   "COSTS ARE FOUND SIMILAR IN NATIONAL
                HEALTH PLANS."
                Rand Corporation report analyzes various
                pending National Health Insurance Plans.
                (p.15)

May 24   "MEDICARE CLIENTS HELD OVERPAYING."
                GAO reports that poor management of
                Medicare results in elderly paying more for
                health costs than they should. (p.60)

June 2   "FEDERAL JOBS BAN FOR ALIENS UPSET."
                U.S. Supreme Court rules it is possible to
                deny supplemental medicare coverage to
                aliens under certain conditions. (p.1)

June 8   "MILLS SEES DEMOCRATIC LOSS IF PARTY
                REJECTS CARTER."
                Congressman Mills predicts passage of
                National Health Insurance within next two
                congressional sessions. (p.30)

July 27   "HEAD OF HEALTH, EDUCATION, WELFARE CITES MEDICARE OVERUSE."
Federal health officials state that overuse of Medicare a severe problem, while fraud isn't. (p.21)

September 23   "ADMINISTRATION BACKS REFORM."
Ford Administration, in significant reversal of policy, endorses legislation to investigate Medicare abuses and fraud. (p.19)

October 1   "RISE OF 19% IN MEDICARE PAYMENTS BY RECIPIENTS SET BY U.S. AGENCY."
Social Security Administration orders 19% increase in payments of Medicare recipients to cover hospital or nursing home costs. Section I. (p.10)

October 25   "SURVEY FINDS MOST NEW YORKERS LIBERAL ON MAJOR DOMESTIC ISSUES."
New York Times poll finds that two-thirds of respondents favor National Health Insurance. (p.1)

December 22   "MEDICARE RECIPIENTS FACE 50-CENT PREMIUM RISE."
50 cents per month rise in Medicare premium will cost recipients $152 million for optimal coverage of doctor bills. (p.14)

January 9, 1977 "NATIONAL HEALTH INSURANCE – THE DREAM WHOSE TIME HAS COME?"
Article on National Health Insurance highlights 6 major proposals. Section F.(p.12)

January 14   "CALIFANO WOULD BAR U.S. AID TO ABORTION."
Health, Education, Welfare Secretary-Designate Joseph A. Califano, Jr., says National Health Insurance remains centerpiece but no legislation introduced in 1977. (p.14)

January 18   "FORD'S PROPOSALS ARE SIMILAR TO CARTER'S IN SUCH AREAS AS HEALTH AND WELFARE REFORM."
President Ford's budget proposals contemplate increase in fees paid by individuals covered by Medicare. (p.20)

122

January 27	"BYRD ASSERTS CARTER LAGS ON ADVICE." Senate Majority Leader Robert C. Byrd says he expects legislation to contain Medicare costs. (p.20)
February 16	"CARTER'S GOALS HINGE ON GROWTH ABOVE 5%, CONGRESS OFFICE SAYS." Congress Budget Office doubts U.S. can afford National Health Insurance; estimated cost $108 billion per year. (p.1)
March 2	"FINANCING MEDICAL CARE." 52% of 23 million Medicare recipients also carry private health insurance to fill gaps left by Medicare. Section C. (p.12)
March 21	"FBI TO INVESTIGATE MEDICAL CARE FRAUD UNTIL HEALTH, EDUCATION, WELFARE SETS UP TEAM." Califano says FBI will investigate Medicare fraud until own resources are operational. (p.23)
April 26	"CARTER PROPOSES LAW FOR TOUGH CONTROLS ON HOSPITAL CHARGES." President Carter's health costs containment legislation indicates National Health Insurance will be delayed several years. (p.1)
May 5	"CALIFANO APOLOGIZES FOR ERRORS IN LISTING." Secretary Califano apologizes to AMA for errors by Health, Education, Welfare in listing of doctors who generated $100,000 or more in Medicare business in 1975. (p.25)
June 15	"MEDICARE FEE RISE CURBED." Health, Education, Welfare announces 6% limit on fee increases for Medicare doctors in year ending 6/30/78. Section B. (p.12)
July 15	"BLUE CROSS IS AWARDED FIRST BID ON MEDICARE." Blue Cross – Blue Shield wins competitive U.S. contract to process Medicare forms of mass recipients; first government action to cut administrative costs. (p.20)

123

August 12   "HUGE INCOMES FOR 6,500 DOCTORS LAID
                 TO QUIRK IN MEDICARE LAW."
                 Nader's Public Citizen's Health Research
                 Group charges that Medicare is subsidizing
                 doctors working in hospital practices by
                 over $100,000; salaries, not fees, should be
                 required. (p.8)
September 14   "MEDICARE PATIENTS TO PAY MORE IN
                 1978."
                 Califano announces Medicare recipients will
                 be required to pay larger share of hospital
                 costs in 1978 due to rising costs; $20 per
                 day up to 60 days or $40 per day above 90
                 days. (p.1)
September 24   "MEDICARE ABUSE BILL IS APPROVED BY
                 HOUSE."
                 House passes legislation with stiffer
                 penalties for provider's fraud. (p.24)
October 30   "HARSHER PENALTIES SET FOR HEALTH
                 CARE FRAUD."
                 Congress passes legislation with stiffer
                 penalties for fraud. (p.58)
November 9   "EFFICACY OF REVIEW BY MEDICAL TEAMS
                 CHALLENGED IN STUDY."
                 Health Services Administration report says
                 PSRO not cost-effective as it is not
                 reducing costs or length of hospital stays.
                 (p.22)
December 11   "OUTLOOK IS GLOOMY ON WELFARE
                 CHANGES."
                 Consensus among congressional and
                 administrative leaders that National Health
                 Insurance will not be enacted by 1980.
                 (p.1)
February 7, 1978 "SOCIAL SECURITY FOCUS OF PLAN FOR
                 TAX RELIEF."
                 Democratic Congress introduces bill to
                 finance health benefits from general
                 revenues rather than solely Social
                 Security. (p.6)
February 28   "BLACK PROGRESS AND POVERTY ARE
                 UNDERLINED BY STATISTICS."
                 New York Times survey of blacks notes
                 that medical care has improved since
                 Medicare and Medicaid. (p.22)

March 1   "CARTER'S URBAN POLICY IS DELAYED,
WITH MAYORS AND GOVERNORS SPLIT."
National Governors Conference shelves
resolution supporting national health
insurance. (p.16)

March 15   "O'NEILL WANTS TO CUT SOCIAL SECURITY
TAX."
Congressman Rostenkowski, chairman of
House Ways and Means Sub-Committee,
opposes funding of Social Security in part
by general revenues as it weakens his
Committee's jurisdiction. (p.21)
"LIST OF BIG MEDICARE FEES CALLED IN
ERROR BY G.A.O."
G.A.O. charges Health, Education, Welfare
list of doctors earning over $100,000 per
year was inaccurate. (p.23)

March 28   "WHITE HOUSE ACKNOWLEDGES TALKS IN
HEALTH INSURANCE LEGISLATION."
Senator Kennedy negotiating with
President Carter to revive National Health
Insurance. (p.28)

April 4   "$ 6 BILLION IS MISSPENT BY HEALTH,
EDUCATION, WELFARE."
Secretary Califano reports $4 billion spent
unnecessarily in health care programs
including Medicare in fiscal 1977; cites
fraud and abuses. (p.18)

April 7   "KENNEDY AND CARTER REACH AN
AGREEMENT ON HEALTH INSURANCE."
Senator Kennedy reports that he, labor
leaders, and President Carter have agreed
on the enactment of National Health
Insurance by 1980; no financing decision
reached. (p.28)

May 12   "HOUSE PANEL VOTES CUT IN TAX
INCREASE FOR SOCIAL SECURITY."
House Committee votes to cut Social
Security taxes. (p.1)

June 21   "CARTER, CALLING TIES WITH SOVIET
STABLE, SAYS TALKS PROGRESS."
President Carter states that administration
is working on National Health Insurance,
but inflation and deficit will postpone
realization for years. (p.1)

October 1 – 2	<u>New York Times</u> on strike. Story abstracted from wire service. No titles given.
October 1	Effects of new federal extending retirement ages on Medicare benefits noted. (p.32)
October 2	Senator Kennedy unveils own national health insurance plan. (p.6)
November 9	"SOCIAL REFORMS AND ARMS ACCORD LIKELY TO FACE SNAG ON CAPITOL HILL." <u>New York Times</u> – <u>CBS</u> poll finds voters support National Health Insurance more than do Congressional candidates. (p.1)
November 15	"AIDES WARN OF CUTS IN PROGRAM GROWTH." Carter Administration official warns Health, Education, Welfare face sharp budget cuts in 1979 budget. (p.15)
November 28	"ELDERLY IN U.S. ARE SOLD UNNEEDED HEALTH INSURANCE AS MEDICARE SUPPLEMENT, CONGRESSIONAL STAFF FINDS." House Committee probes insurance fraud of Medicare supplement. (p.16)
December 8	"LIBERALS PRESS FLOOR FIGHTS BEFORE DEMOCRATIC PARLEY." Analysis of liberal Democrats and Carter Administration on outstanding legislation including National Health Insurance is presented. (p.21)
December 10	"KENNEDY ASSAILS CARTER ON BUDGET AT MIDTERM MEETING OF DEMOCRATS." Senator Kennedy and President Carter openly disagree on National Health Insurance. (p.1)
December 17	"RX FOR HEALTH CARE: THE COST IS STAGGERING." Analysis of costs of different national health insurance plans presented. Section D. (p.4)
December 31	"MOST NEAR 65 ARE EXPECTED TO RETIRE VOLUNTARILY." Medicare deductible increases by 11% as well as cost of co-insurance. (p.20)

126

January 19, 1979   "OUTLOOK ON HEALTH BUDGET."
President Carter will reportedly propose eliminating Medicare payments for chiropractors and others to hold costs down in 1980 budget. (p.11)

January 23   "SOCIAL PROGRAMS: MANY FACE SUBSTANTIAL DECREASES."
President Carter, in proposed budget, calls hospital cost containment as most urgent economy step. (p.12)

January 24   "CARTER PUSHES FOR ARMS PACT AND INFLATION CURB TO SET NEW FOUNDATION."
President Carter, in State of Union Address, proposes development of national health plan. (p.12)

January 31   "CARTER BUDGET GETS SUPPORT IN SURVEY."
New York Times poll finds little public support for all-out effort in National Health Insurance. (p.1)

March 23   "CARTER TO PROPOSE A $10 BILLION PLAN ON HEALTH FOR 1983."
President Carter plans to ask Congress within next few months to approve phase I of national health insurance that would cost $10-$15 billion beginning in 1983. (p.1)

March 28   "CALIFANO GIVES MORE DETAILS ON CARTER HEALTH PLAN."
Secretary Califano explains how Carter plan will work. (p.21)

May 6   "NEW, VARIED PRESCRIPTIONS PUSH A NATIONAL HEALTH PLAN."
Analysis of various congressional plans for national health insurance. Section D. (p.5)

June 1   "U.S. LISTS THE DOCTORS CONVICTED FOR FRAUDS IN MEDICARE - MEDICAID."
Federal government releases for first time, names of health providers who have been convicted of defrauding Medicare. (p.19)

June 6

"HEALTH PLAN OF CARTER IS REPORTED TO COVER MEDICAL CATASTROPHES."
President Carter will propose a national health insurance focusing on catastrophic coverage. Section D (p.17)

June 13

"CARTER AND KENNEDY PRESS RIVAL EFFORTS ON HEALTH PROGRAM."
President Carter and Senator Kennedy marshal support for opposing national health insurance plans. (p.1)

October 14

"MEDICARE PATIENTS TO PAY MORE FOR HOSPITAL TREATMENT IN 1980."
Health, Education, Welfare increases Medicare hospital insurance deductible from $160 to $180 beginning 1/80; patients share of hospital per diem after 60 days will also increase. (p.52)

October 21

"PANEL MAY ASK ROLLBACK OF SOCIAL SECURITY TAXES."
Federal advisory panel proposes financing hospital part of Medicare from earmarked income taxes rather than Social Security payroll taxes. (p.26)

November 25

"STUDY LINKS HIGHER FEES TO DOCTOR-INSURER TIES."
FTC study links higher doctor bills to doctors' control of nation's Blue Cross Insurance plans. (p.51)

December 2

"RULE ON PAYMENTS BY MEDICARE FOR NON-COVERED SERVICES CLARIFIED."
Health, Education, Welfare says Medicare beneficiaries must pay for non-covered services only if their doctors give them written notice in advance that government will not pay for procedure. (p.59)

December 20

"U.S., IN TEST PROJECT, TO PAY CARE OF SOME DYING."
U.S. government will pay all costs for dying patients in hospice under Medicare as part of two-year experiment. (p.22)

January 20, 1980   "CARTER IS EXPECTED TO SEEK FUND SHIFT ON SOCIAL SECURITY."
President Carter is expected to ask Congress for authority to borrow from Disability and Medicare trust funds in order to augment Social Security funds. (p.1)

January 29   "CARTER BUDGET MESSAGE AND MAJOR PROPOSALS."
Summary of President Carter's budget plans in health care. (p.9)

March 2   "HOW MEDICARE AND MEDICAID WORK."
Explanation of how Medicare and Medicaid work. Section K. (p.17)

March 23   "STUDY CRITICIZES CANCER INSURANCE."
House Select Committee on Aging scores sales tactics to sell cancer insurance to Medicare patients. (p.50)

"U.S. SEEKS NEW REPORTS TO CURB HOSPITAL COSTS."
Federal government proposes uniform reporting standards for 7,000 hospitals that serve Medicare and Medicaid patients in effort to diminish wide disparities in hospital costs; industry council scores proposal. (p.45)

June 21   "SENATOR INTRODUCES BILL TO ALLOW SOCIAL SECURITY PLAN TO BORROW."
Senator Packwood introduces legislation allowing President to borrow from disability and health insurance to protect pension fund. (p.8)

July 25   "AMA, UNDER PRESSURE, MOVING TO ACCEPT CHANGE."
New AMA president cites medical acceptance of Medicaid and Medicare as evidence of decreasing conservatism of AMA; credits two federal programs with increasing access of 38% of Americans to medical care. (p.1)

August 18   "PARTIES' PLATFORMS: THE CONTRASTS ON ISSUES."
Article summarizes how Republican and Democratic parties differ on major social and economic issues. (p.14)

| August 31 | "ANDERSON OFFERS A PLATFORM THAT URGES VOTERS TO PUT NATION OVER PARTY." |

August 31   "ANDERSON OFFERS A PLATFORM THAT URGES VOTERS TO PUT NATION OVER PARTY."
Independent presidential candidate John B. Anderson platform includes efforts to deter over-utilization and waste by Medicare and Medicaid patients. (p.20)

September 5   "HOUSE VOTES, 294-91, FOR $9 BILLION PLAN TO RECONCILE BUDGET."
House approves Medicare and Medicaid funds bill that adjusts procedures for advance hospital payments. (p.1)

September 29   "FLORIDA DOCTORS FOUND TO CHARGE ELDERLY 100% MARKUPS FOR TESTS."
Unpublished GAO report says elderly pay more in Florida because doctors are charging more than 100% over cost for lab procedures. Sections D. (p.10)

November 17   "HOUSE COMMITTEE SAYS MEDICARE LOSES $2 BILLION A YEAR TO FRAUD."
Unreleased report of House Select Committee on Aging charges that Medicare program loses $2 billion to fraud. (p.16)

December 18   "CONSUMER REPORT ON MEDICARE FINDS ELDERLY PAY BULK OF COSTS."
Public Citizen Health Research Group study finds that Medicare, on the average, pays less than 30 cents on the dollar of each Medicare bill. (p.28)

January 7, 1981   "THREE CABINET CHOICES BREEZE THROUGH SENATE HEARINGS."
Richard S. Schweiker, Health and Human Services Secretary designate, says comprehensive national health insurance is out of question. (p.16)

January 16   "CARTER SEEKS NEW INDEX TO CURB SOARING BENEFITS."
President Carter budget proposal estimates $7 billion increase in Medicare costs to $47 billion. Section B. (p.7)

130

February 9   "LETTING MARKET FORCES HELP GOVERN
               PROVISION OF HEALTH CARE."
               Article by Sam Allalouf arguing that
               competition among health care providers is
               needed to contain rising Medicare costs.
               (p.1)
February 11   "REAGAN WON'T CUT SEVEN SOCIAL
               PROGRAMS THAT AID 80 MILLION."
               Medicare is one of programs exempted
               from President Reagan's proposed budget
               cuts for fiscal 1982. (p.1)
February 16   "MEDICAL LEADERS GROWING WARY OVER
               REAGAN HEALTH-CARE PLANS."
               AMA defends Medicare against proposed
               cutbacks being considered by Reagan staff.
               (p.12)
February 19   "THREE EX-OFFICIAL SUPPORT TAPPING
               INCOME TAX TO FINANCE MEDICARE."
               Three former Social Security
               Commissioners agree that Medicare should
               be financed by tax revenues rather than
               payroll taxes. (p.26)
March 13   "CENSUS FINDS U.S. BENEFITS REACH 1
               OUT OF 3 FAMILIES."
               Analyses of Census Bureau on number and
               characteristics of Medicare recipients.
               (p.12)
March 13   "DIVIDED U.S. ADVISORY PANEL URGES
               CHANGES IN SOCIAL SECURITY SYSTEM."
               U.S. Advisory Committee makes
               recommendation that half of Medicare be
               funded by general tax revenues. (p.15)
March 11   "REAGAN 'SOCIAL SECURITY NET'
               PROPOSAL: WHO WILL LAND, WHO WILL
               FALL THROUGH."
               Analysis of Medicare recipients focusing on
               those earning more than $30,000 and
               receiving benefits. Section B. (p.10)
March 19   "SENATE UNIT SPEEDS SHARP BUDGET
               CUTS SOUGHT BY REAGAN."
               Senate Budget Committee votes to cut
               Medicare and Medicaid by $200 million
               more than proposed by Reagan. (p.1)

March 30   "PENSION LAWS SOUGHT TO AVERT SOCIAL SECURITY GAP."
            Congressman Pepper drafts five-year plan to have part of Medicare financed by general tax revenues. Section B. (p.11)

April 2   "KEY G.O.P. SENATORS SEEK CUTS IN UNTOUCHED MEDICARE PROGRAM."
            Senators Dole and Durenberger (Chairman of Senate Finance Committee), want to cut Medicare program by $1 billion. Section B. (p.11)

April 5   "CONGRESS HITS SNAG ON SOCIAL SECURITY."
            Congressional impasse over Medicare funding as to how to finance the program. (p.25)

May 13   "U.S. IS SUING A MEDICAL SUPPLIER."
            U.S. government sues Medical equipment company for $200,000 in Medicare overcharges. (p.4)

June 27   "HOUSE BUDGET CUTS DIFFER FROM COMMITTEE VERSION."
            Comparison of Reagan proposals and congressional bills that passed one or both houses dealing with aspects of Medicare. (p.8)

June 28   "MEDICARE COSTS GET CUT."
            Medicare is 15 years old. Estimated expenditures for next five years are presented. Section C (p.1)

July 7   "FISCAL CRISIS FOR MEDICARE BY 1990 PREDICTED BY THREE OFFICERS OF CABINET."
            Secretaries Regan, Donovan, and Schweiker believe that congressional action of fee increases has only made Medicare solvent for eight to ten more years. (p.1)

July 12   "DON'T THROW OUT THE BABY WITH MEDICAID - MEDICARE BATHWATER."
            Article explaining why Medicare and Medicaid should be continued despite financial problems. Section D (p.22)

132

July 29   "MAJOR PROVISIONS OF THE BUDGET BILL
           AGREED TO BY SENATE AND HOUSE
           CONFEREES."
           Summary article on proposed Medicare
           legislative changes. (p.18)
August 13 "MEDICARE ALTERNATIVE STUDIED."
           Reagan Administration considering voucher
           system for Medicare. Section D. (p.20)
October 31 "U.S. REPORT SAYS INCREASE IN HEALTH
           SPENDING IS BIGGEST IN 15 YEARS."
           Medicare cost $61 billion in 1980 says
           health care financing agency representing
           28% of total health bill in U.S. Medicare
           costs rose 21.4%. (p.19)
November 8 "REAGAN AIDES MAP PROPOSALS TO CUT
           HEALTH CARE COSTS."
           Secretary Schweiker proposes new limits to
           Medicare and Medicaid to control costs;
           plans outlined. (p.1)
November 14 "SOCIAL SECURITY LAGGING BADLY ON
           PAY RECORDS."
           Social Security Administration lagging
           behind in recording workers' earnings,
           which endangers individual Medicare
           benefits. (p.1)
December 4 "WHITE HOUSE AGING POLICY ADOPTS
           AGENDA FOR DECADE."
           White House Conference on Aging calls for
           no cuts in Medicare or Medicaid;
           establishment of national health insurance.
           (p.18)
December 10 "DOCTOR CALLS MEDICARE PLAN EASY TO
           DEFRAUD."
           Cardiologist pleads guilty to filing $1.5
           million false Medicare claims; doctor calls
           system vulnerable. (p.28)
December 24 "1983 BUDGET IS NEAR COMPLETION:
           DEFICIT MAY EXCEED $100 BILLION."
           Reagan calls for cuts in Medicare in fiscal
           1983 budget. Section B. (p.4)
December 30 "INSURANCE PREMIUM RISING."
           Medicare's supplementary program to
           increase to $12.20 per month; an 11.2%
           increase. Section D. (p.14)

January 9, 1982   "MEDICARE PATIENTS MAY BE FORCED TO PAY 10% OF HOSPITAL CHARGES."
Reagan Administration considers proposals to have Medicare recipients pay 10% of hospital costs up to $2500. (p.11)

January 15   "COALITION SEEKS TO CURB RISING HEALTH CARE COST."
AMA, Blue Cross and Blue Shield, Business Roundtable, HIP, and AFL-CIO agree on the need to control health care costs: voluntary coalition formed despite past disagreements. (p.10)

January 23   "FROM THE 'TRULY NEEDY,' A CRY FOR THAT ELUSIVE 'SAFETY NET.'"
Labor Department reports that medical costs rose 12.5% in 1981, largest since World War II. (p.1)

January 27   "REAGAN VOWS TO KEEP TAX CUTS. PROPOSES $47 BILLION TRANSFER OF SOCIAL PROGRAMS TO STATES."
In State of Union message, President proposes to give up responsibility for food stamp program in return for control over Medicare and Medicaid. (p.1)

January 29   "U.S. PLAN STIRS FEAR."
Analysis of Reagan swap idea and comments of New York City officials. Section B. (p.1)

February 2   "THE NEW STATES RIGHTS."
Tom Wicker column on Reagan swap. (p.25)

February 5   "REAGAN REPORTED ASKING BENEFIT CUT."
Reagan reportedly planning to cut Medicare and Medicaid funding by $5 billion in next year's budget. (p.18)

February 8   "REPORT ON HEALTH CARE FINDS PATTERN OF BIAS."
National Academy of Sciences reports that blacks and minorities often need health care more and receive less care and usually lower quality. (p.14)

134

February 9	"CONCERN VOICED IN CABINET OVER 'NEW FEDERATION.'" Federal control over Medicare and Medicaid worries Secretary Schweiker as it could be basis for national health insurance. (p.6)
March 3	"CRITICS SAY REAGAN MEDICARE CUTS WOULD ONLY SHIFT HOSPITAL COSTS." Two percent across the board cuts in Medicare funding to hospitals will not save money says coalition group. (p.21)
March 15	"U.S. TO USE COMPUTERS IN MORE FRAUD DETECTION." Health and Human Services plans nationwide search for Medicare and Medicaid fraud. (p.12)
March 19	"STUDIES OF WELFARE CUTS ASSESS HARM TO ELDERLY." House Select Committee on Aging reports that Reagan proposals will increase costs for elderly so that Medicare and Medicaid reductions are made up. (p.20)
March 27	"PANEL SAYS MOST STATES FAIL ON POLICING MEDICAID FRAUD." House Select Committee on Aging report concludes that Health and Human Services and most states do poor job in monitoring Medicare; only New York State considered doing good job. (p.9)
March 28	"HIGH MEDICAL COSTS UNDER ATTACK AS DRAIN ON THE NATION'S ECONOMY." Review article charges that fee for service gives doctors and hospitals a blank check to raise Medicare costs. (p.1)
April 7	"WHITE HOUSE HALTS ATTEMPT TO SHIFT WELFARE TO STATES." Reagan swap ideas fails to secure support; Reagan gives up. (p.1)
April 20	"HOSPITAL INDUSTRY PROPOSES FIXED PAYMENTS FOR MEDICARE PATIENTS." Hospital Association calls for standard payment for hospital costs under Medicare. Section B. (p.6)

April 24	"INSURANCE TO BOLSTER MEDICARE." Different supplemental plans for Medicare are analyzed. (p.12)
July 27	"1981 SPENDING FOR HEALTH CARE IS UP BY 15.1%." Health and Human Service reports American spent $287 billion for health care in 1981; represents 9.8% of gross national produce. (p.1)
August 4	"MEDICARE VOUCHER PLAN GETS SUPPORT FROM REAGAN OFFICIAL." Reagan Administration endorses Medicare voucher plan to increase competition and hold costs down. Section B. (p.7)
August 12	"ADMINISTRATION LAG CITED IN SOURING HEALTH COSTS." Article on health care costs indicating that they have risen twice as fast as the CPI. Section B. (p.12)
September 19	"U.S. IS STUDYING LIMIT ON INCOME UNDER MEDICARE." Federal officials report that the Office of Budget and Management is studying proposals to have elderly demonstrate need before receiving Medicare. (p.1)
September 21	"SCHWEIKER ASSAILS CURB ON MEDICARE." Secretary Schweiker states opposition to Office of Budget and Management proposals. (p.22)
October 1	"BENEFIT CHANGES TAKE EFFECT TODAY." Medicare program is expected to cost $55 billion in 1983 despite Congress action to reduce growth by $2.8 billion. (p.21)
October 7	"U.S. MOVING TO FIX UNIFORM FEE SCALE ON MEDICARE CASES." Secretary Schweiker proposes that Medicare pays all hospitals the same amount, fixed in advance, for treating patients with particular diagnosis. (p.1)
October 8	"MEDICARE PAYMENT PROPOSAL BY U.S. HAILED AND ATTACKED." Reactions to DRG are outlined. Section B. (p.3)
October 12	"WHO WILL PAY WHAT FOR HEALTH CARE?" Analysis of DRG is presented. (p.24)

136

November 23	"LAWMAKERS CHALLENGE PLANNED MEDICARE SHIFT." Congressional hearings on DRG are held; mixed reviews. (p.25)
December 19	"HOW POOR ARE THE ELDERLY?" Article analyzing relationship between elderly and Social Security and Medicare. Section C. (p.4)
December 25	"PRESIDENTIAL SHIFT ON JOBS PREDICTED." Summary of actions taken in Second Session of 97th Congress. (p.5)
December 31	"SCHWEIKER PROPOSES TO RELAX FEDERAL REGULATIONS OF SMALL HOSPITALS." Health and Human Services formally proposes to reduce number of requirements that hospitals must satisfy to become a Medicare participant. (p.10)
January 1, 1983	"TOP HEALTH OFFICIAL URGES PER-ILLNESS MEDICARE FEES." Secretary Schweiker proposes setting uniform rates for hospital fees for Medicare patients, which accounts for 26.6% of $118 billion spent on hospital care in 1981. (p.1)
January 24	"HEALTH CARE COSTS UP 11%, NEARLY TRIPLE INFLATION RATE." Medicare costs increasing at 11% rate in 1982, or three times as much as rest of indicators in CPI. (p.8)
January 29	"REAGAN PROPOSING $848.5 BILLION BUDGET." President Reagan's budget proposals outline changes in Medicare including freezing doctors' fees and having elderly pay share of routing hospital costs. (p.6)
February 3	"REAGAN MEDICARE PROPOSALS ARE BROADLY CRITICIZED." President Reagan's Medicare proposals are criticized by the American Public Health Association at a hearing of Senate Finance Committee. (p.19)

February 21	"BY 1989 MEDICARE WILL USE UP FUND. TWO U.S. REPORTS SAY." Congressional Budget Office predicts that Medicare trust fund will be depleted in 1987 or 1988 if Social Security fails to pay interest on $12.4 billion borrowed from Medicare. (p.1)
February 22	"STRICTER AUDITS URGED FOR MEDICARE – MEDICAID." General Accounting Office releases study indicating Medicare audit of providers' charges are poor, resulting in unneeded medical costs. (p.13)
February 23	"HOUSE PANEL VOTES FIXED PAYMENTS FOR MEDICARE." House Ways and Means Sub-Committee on Health approves Reagan's DRG Proposals. (p.13)
March 1	"REAGAN ASKING WIDE CHANGES IN NATIONS'S HEALTH INSURANCE SYSTEM." President Reagan proposes that Medicare provides coverage for catastrophic illnesses that require long hospital stays. (p.17)
April 10	"MEDICARE PROPOSALS SAID TO BURDEN THOSE MOST ILL." Congressional Budget Office warns that proposals to increase charges for Medicare services to elderly who already pay large amounts for hospital stay and physician services will increase the burden to those most ill.. (p.28)
April 15	"SENATE PANEL WARNED ABOUT MEDICARE DEFICIT." CBO warns that Medicare fund will be bankrupt by 1988. (p.16)
May 2	"U.S. ACTS TO CUT BENEFIT TO DYING IN HOSPICE CARE." Reagan Administration drafts rules to reduce Hospice payments under Medicare to 60% of Congressional levels. (p.1)
May 26	"HOUSE PANEL ON AGING ASSAILS DRAFT RULES ON HOSPICE COSTS." Congressmen from both parties criticize Reagan Administration plan to reduce Hospice payment. (p.20)

June 24   "REAGAN ASKS DOCTORS TO SUPPORT FREEZE IN THEIR MEDICARE RETURNS."
Reagan proposes one-year freeze in Medicare payments to doctors. Section D (p.14)

June 25   "MEDICARE ANALYSIS PREDICTS INSOLVENCY OF THE FUND BY 1990."
Reagan Administration reports that Medicare trust fund is facing insolvency around 1990. (p.1)

July 19   "MEDICAL PAYMENTS RISE 12.5% IN 1982."
Health and Human Service reports that in 1983, Medicare and Medicaid payments were about $83 billion. Section B. (p.7)

August 25   "MEDICARE EXPERTS REJECT EXCISE TAX."
Federal Advisory Committee rejects increasing taxes on alcohol and tobacco for helping to finance Medicare programs. (p.15)

August 28   "HOSPITALS WORRY OVER FIXED RATE SET FOR MEDICARE."
Officials of U.S. hospitals fear new Medicare prospective payment system will make it more difficult for some patients to obtain treatment. (p.1)

September 1   "STANDARD RATES SET FOR HOSPITALS UNDER MEDICARE."
Health and Human Services Secretary Heckler announces first big step toward standard nationwide rates for hospitals treating patients under Medicare program. (p.1)

September 4   "MEDICARE: THE NEXT CRISIS OVER ENTITLEMENT."
Review article outlining best and worst scenario on financing Medicare. Section D. (p.6)

September 7   "CHANGES DUE FOR HOSPITALS."
Changes in Medicare hospital reimbursement should slow rate of earnings of hospital management companies. Section D. (p.8)

September 25	"HOSPITAL RATES: CRITICISM RISES AS U.S. SHIFTS." Limitation of hospital payment under Medicare begins on September 29th. Section K. (p.1)
October 2	"CHANGES IN MEDICARE SEEK TO CONTROL COSTS." Article reviews difficulties that Health and Human Services is having in trying to cost-contain Medicare and Medicaid programs. Section D. (p.4)
November 5	"MEDICARE ADVISORY UNIT SEEKING MAJOR CHANGES." Federal Advisory Committee votes to raise age of eligibility to 67 and increase premiums paid by beneficiaries as steps to avert Medicare bankruptcy. (p.12)
November 30	"VAST REFORM NEEDED TO SAVE MEDICARE, STUDY SAYS." Congressional Budget Office says incremental approach will not succeed in protecting Medicare; massive restructuring needed. (p.27)
December 11	"ADMINISTRATION SETS PAYMENT RATES FOR HOSPICES UNDER MEDICARE." Secretary Heckler announces regulations setting payment rates for hospice care. (p.60)
January 5, 1984	"REAGAN BUDGET SAID TO INCLUDE MEDICARE SHIFT." Reagan will ask Congress to revise Medicare program so that it will become a catastrophic illness protection program that would pay all hospital costs after two months. (p.1)
January 7	"HEALTH COST CURB ASKED BY MONDALE." Mondale proposes federal spending limits for hospital care and physician services. (p.8)

January 17   "REAGAN SAID TO OPPOSE PANEL ON
                    PARING DEFICITS."
                    Reagan reportedly decides against plan to
                    cut Medicare costs by having patients pay
                    more for short hospital stays in exchange
                    for better average costs of long-term
                    illness. Section D. (p.24)

January 29   "INCREASE IN HEALTH CARE COST FOUND
                    SLOWING."
                    Bureau of Labor Statistics report shows
                    rate of increase for health care in 1983
                    was lowest since 1973. Strain on Medicare
                    trust fund eases. (p.20)

February 17   "OUTLOOK IS BRIGHTER FOR MEDICARE
                    TRUST FUND, AGENCY SAYS."
                    CBO report concludes that Medicare trust
                    fund is in better shape than earlier
                    expected – will be O.K. through 1989.
                    (p.15)

February 20   "LINKING MEDICARE AND ABILITY TO PAY."
                    Review article analyzing arguments for and
                    against "Means Test" in Medicare program.
                    Congress plans no action in an election
                    year. (p.11)

March 5   "CHRYSLER HARD HIT BY COSTS, STUDIES
                    HEALTH CARE SYSTEM."
                    Chrysler Corporation chairman Iacocca
                    claims American companies will go
                    bankrupt unless nation's system of health
                    care is revamped. Workers resist paying
                    higher share for Medicare. (p.1)

March 11   "PANEL URGES RAISING AGE FOR
                    MEDICARE PLAN TO 67."
                    Federal Advisory Council on Social
                    Security recommends increasing eligibility
                    age to 67, taxing employer-paid health
                    insurance benefits, etc., to be able to
                    arrange coverage for catastrophic illness.
                    (p.23)

April 2   "MEDICARE TO ADJUST PAYMENTS."
                    Secretary Heckler says Medicare payment
                    scheduled for hospitals will be changed
                    next year to meet criticism focused on
                    local wage rates and urban-rural
                    differences. Section D. (p.13)

April 6   "SOCIAL SECURITY FUND REPORTED FINANCIALLY SOUND."
Reagan Administration report states Medicare Trust Fund solvent until 1991. Either reduce outlays or income must be raised to insure continued solvency. (p.14)

April 13   "HOUSE VOTES CUTS IN BENEFIT PLANS TO REDUCE DEFICIT."
One year freeze on doctors' fees paid by Medicare is defeated in House of Representatives. (p.1)

April 16   "HOSPITAL MERGERS INCREASE AID COST, U.S. STUDIES FIND."
Federal officials contend hospital mergers are rapidly increasing Medicare costs without improving services to elderly. (p.1)

April 29   "SOME ERRANT DOCTORS GET NEW U.S. FUNDS BY CHANGING STATES."
GAO report criticizes lack of central registry for barred physicians who are able to set up practice in different state and collect Medicare. (p.1)

May 22   "JUSTICES ALLOW U.S. TO RECOUP OVERPAYMENT DESPITE MISTAKE."
U.S. Supreme Court rules that government can recover overpayment of federal funds from recipient who relied on mistaken advice. (p.18)

May 27   "HEALTH AND MEDICINE."
Medicare demonstration HMO in New Jersey is launched; hopes to save money. Section K. (p.14)

June 10   "STATE GETS NEW DRG RATE DEADLINE."
Federal officials will switch from New Jersey to U.S. DRG payment system in New Jersey unless latter can prove savings. Section K. (p.4)

June 22   "HEALTH SPENDING CUTS APPROVED: CONFEREES BREAK 3-DAY DEADLOCK."
House and Senate tax conferees agree on 15-month freeze on doctors' fees under Medicare. (p.1)

June 23	"MEDICAL GROUPS OBJECT TO MEDICARE FEE PLAN."
	Opposition to doctors' fees freeze voiced by national and state medical societies. (p.9)
June 28	"CONGRESS APPROVES TAX RISE."
	House and Senate pass 4-year tax increase; most spending cuts occur in Medicare. Section D. (p.13)
August 4	"MEW MEDICARE PLAN FAULTED."
	Researchers believe DRG in Medicare will result in more shorter stays resulting in greater, not less, financial outlays by feds. (p.28)
August 26	"MEDICARE LIMITS MAKE HOSPITALS CAREFUL ON COSTS."
	Health officials in U.S. report that hospitals are more cost efficient due to DRG, and average length of hospital stay has declined dramatically. (p.1)
September 23	"DOCTORS' GROUP SUES TO HALT FREEZE ON MEDICARE PAYMENT."
	AMA sues to block new freeze on doctors' Medicare fees. (p.41)
September 30	"MEDICAID FEE FREEZE TO START."
	Federal Judge Sarah E. Baker rules against AMA. (p.25)
	"MEDICARE PATIENTS' COST TO RISE."
	Health and Human Services reports that hospital deductible under Medicare to rise to $400 from $356. (p.25)
October 1	"U.S. IMPOSES FREEZE ON PHYSICIANS' MEDICARE FEES."
	Medicare will impose one year freeze on payments for doctors starting October 1st. Section B. (p.12)
October 7	"ACCOUNTS LIKE I.R.A. IS PROPOSED FOR HEALTH."
	Heritage Foundation report suggests that Medicare should be replaced with people being allowed to put money into tax-exempt health accounts for retirement. (p.,54)

October 19   "THE CHECK IS IN THE MAIL."
                  Health and Human Services official
                  recommends that Medicare not pay bills
                  promptly, as $1 billion could be saved in
                  five years. (p.24)

October 28   "SOCIAL SECURITY SURPLUS SEEN AS A
                  MEDICARE AID."
                  Senator Moynihan advises use of Social
                  Security surplus to bail out Medicare trust.
                  (p.45)

November 10   "TOXIC WASTE BILL SIGNED BY REAGAN."
                  President Reagan signs into law increasing
                  Medicare payment rate for hospice. (p.7)

November 14   "PLAN FOR MEDICARE WOULD PUT DOCTOR
                  ON PER-ILLNESS FEE."
                  Health and Human Services considering flat
                  all-inclusive rate to doctors for care of
                  patient in hospital. (p.1)

December 2   "MEDICARE REVIEW STIR CONCERN."
                  Federal officials can deny doctors payment
                  for what they deem is unnecessary
                  surgery. (p.1)
                  "HEALTH-CARE PROVIDERS BARRED FROM
                  MEDICARE."
                  Health and Human Services removes more
                  than 300 doctors and medical suppliers
                  from Medicare program due to fraudulent
                  claims. (p.40)

December 14   "IN-HOSPITAL SURGERY TO BE REDUCED
                  BY CONTRACTS TO SAVE ON MEDICARE."
                  New federal regulations for Medicare will
                  result in greater utilization of outpatient
                  services. (p.1)

December 29   "OFFICIALS ATTACK MEDICARE FREEZE."
                  Health care officials warn that extending
                  freeze on Medicare payments for doctors
                  will affect negatively the quality of
                  service. (p.7)

January 8, 1985   "NEW TAXING FOR MEDICARE PROPOSED."
                  Secretary Heckler has proposed the use of
                  part of the federal excise tax on
                  cigarettes to be earmarked for the
                  Medicare's Hospital Insurance Trust Fund.
                  (p.14)

January 10   "MEDICARE TO PAY HEALTH GROUPS IN ADVANCE."
              New Medicare regulations permit advance payments for health groups. (p.9)

January 13   "KEAN HAILS HOSPITAL ACCORD."
              Governor Kean states that the impact of the new Medicare waiver will be favorable for the New Jersey DRG system. Section B. (p.9)

January 20   "WASHINGTON DRIVES A HARD BARGAIN ON MEDICAL COSTS; SOME HOSPITALS COULD BE HURTING."
              Articles analyze the impact of the DRG's on hospitals and the ability to serve the poor. Section D. (p.3)

February 5   "EXTENSIVE CUTBACKS OFFERED IN HEALTH AID AND SUBSIDIES."
              President Reagan's budget message proposes new restraints on Medicare. (p.17)

March 3   "STATE FEARS REAGAN BID TO CUT HEALTH AID."
              New Jersey officials criticize President Reagan's proposed Medicare restraints. Section B. (p.1)

March 8   "ELDERLY SEE SHARE OF HOSPITAL COSTS RISE."
              HCFA analyzes hospital costs and how much is paid for by Medicare recipients. (p.16)

March 28   "MEDICARE REPORT MORE OPTIMISTIC."
              Medicare trust fund predicted to be solvent until the late 1990's. Section D. (p.30)

April 9   "REVIEW BARS 13.9% OF PAYMENTS BY MEDICARE TO HOSPITALS IN CITY."
              Medicare review disallows payments for prolonged service. (p.1)

May 4   "SENATE APPROVES CUTS IN SPENDING ON HEALTH CARE."
              The Senate voted to cut Medicare and Medicaid health care programs by $17.5 billion over 3 years. (p.10)

May 20	"MEDICAL CARE PLANS CREATED IN THE 60'S KEEP WIDE SUPPORT." Bipartisan support for Medicare is analyzed. (p.1)
May 29	"U.S. PLANS TO FREEZE MEDICARE HOSPITAL PAYMENTS." HCFA freezes 1986 hospital payments. (p.1)
June 9	"DEBATE IS GROWING OVER MEDICARE AID." Reagan officials oppose differential rates for hospitals serving the poor. (p.33)
July 2	"MEDICARE PAYMENTS RAISED FOR HOSPITALS SERVING POOR." Health and Human services adopts new rules authorizing larger payments for hospitals serving the poor. (p.12)
July 6	"FURTHER MEDICAL CUTS MADE; SAVING IS PUT AT $225 MILLION." Health and Human Services implements a plan to reduce aid to medical education via Medicare. (p.8)
July 21	"MEDICARE ASSAILED ON HOME-CARE CAP." New strict Medicare rules limit payments for home health care. Section B. (p.1)
August 2	"COMPROMISE AVOIDS MAJOR CUTS IN BENEFITS." Congressional conferees agree on Medicare budget. (p.9)
August 3	"DEFICIT PROJECTIONS IN NEW BUDGET TOO OPTIMISTIC, CONGRESSMEN SAY." Analysis of President's proposal, House, Senate, and Compromise Plan is presented. (p.8)
August 23	"CONGRESS WILL GET PLAN TO EVEN OUT FEES FOR MEDICARE." Health and Human Services proposing new fee schedules for doctors. (p.1)
August 24	"RX FOR FEES: U.S. OUTLOOK." Health policy experts analyze proposed fee schedules. (p.29)

October 25	"HOSPITAL STAYS SHORTER, MEDICARE REPORT SAYS."
	Congressional report finds that the DRG's have reduced average length of hospital stay. Premature to indicate whether quality is affected. (p.18)
November 23	"MEDICARE BACKS NEW DIAGNOSTIC TECHNIQUE."
	Medicare agrees to pay for the diagnostic procedure known as magnetic resonance imaging. (p.28)
November 28	"HOSPITAL PROFITS CLIMB IN NEW MEDICARE PLAN."
	A survey of 892 hospitals in nine states revealed the hospitals to have a 14.12% increase in Medicare revenue over the previous year. Section B. (p.9)
December 15	"REAGAN'S BUDGET FOR 1987 SEEKING MEDICARE SAVINGS."
	Office of Management and Budget proposes plan to reduce Medicare fees for doctors. (p.1)
December 21	"NEW SECRETARY FIGHTS MEDICARE CUTS."
	Secretary Bowen fights to restore cuts in Medicare. (p.12)
January 16, 1986	"PUBLIC EXPECTED TO SEE VARIOUS SMALL EFFECTS IN FEDERAL PROGRAMS."
	Doctors will receive less for treating older Medicare patients; resulting from automatic budget cuts as part of new budget-balancing law. (p.1)
January 20	"DISCIPLINARY CASES RISE FOR DOCTORS."
	Federally financed review agencies have begun disciplinary action against 1100 doctors and hospitals for providing unnecessary or poor medical treatment. (p.1)
February 4	"REAGAN'S BUDGET ASKING CUTBACKS IN HEALTH PLANS."
	Five year cut of $70 billion being proposed in projected spending for Medicare and Medicaid. (p.1)

April 1   "BOARD PREDICTS MEDICARE BANKRUPTCY."
The Federal Trust Fund Board of Directors predicts bankruptcy could occur in 1996 if no action is taken. Section B. (p.20)

June 18   "U.S. EASES RULES FOR HOSPITALS."
New rules are issued that will ease the administrative burdens required of rural hospitals. (p.24)

June 19   "AMA DELEGATES SEEK TO REPLACE MEDICARE."
Policy makers propose to replace Medicare at annual convention. (p.9)

June 28   "HEART TRANSPLANT COSTS TO BE PAID BY MEDICARE."
Medicare issues rules indicating it will pay the bills incurred in heart transplants. (p.6)

November 2   "AGENCY ASKING U.S. CARE IN 'CATASTROPHIC ILLS.'"
Health and Human Services drafting a report expanding Medicare to include covering long, severe illness. (p.1)

November 21   "BOWEN PROPOSES CATASTROPHIC ILLNESS COVERAGE."
Secretary Bowen adopts recommendation of staff and urges expansion of Medicare to cover long, severe illness. (p.1)

December 3   "PROPOSAL WOULD TAP SOCIAL SECURITY PAYMENTS."
Government report recommends unpaid hospital co-payment bills be deducted from the beneficiaries' monthly payment. (p.24)

December 6   "PLAN WOULD CURB FEES OF PHYSICIANS PAID BY MEDICARE."
Plan would combine payment of hospital and doctor into one payment which would be less than the two separate payments. (p.1)

December 9   "BOWEN PROTESTS REAGAN PLAN TO CUT HEALTH BUDGET."
Secretary Bowen opposes plan to combine payments for physicians and hospitals into one lump sum. (p.20)

December 26   "AMA SUIT ALLEGES BIAS IN NEW RULES
                   ON MEDICARE FEES."
                       Suit alleges that rules which impose
                   penalties for the elderly using doctors who
                   charge more than government set fees is
                   unconstitutional.   (p.1)

Name Index

149

152

George L. Maddox   58
Charlotte Mahoney   34
Michael Mansfield   119
Kenneth Manton   70
Theodore R. Marmor   37, 58
Robert J. Master   58
Sarah H. Matthews   58
George Meany   98
R.E. Merritt   59
Dulcy B. Miller   59
Wilbur Mills   8, 81, 83,
   89, 102, 111, 113, 120
Meredith Minkler   32, 59
Janet B. Mitchell   60
Walter Mondale   106, 139
Rhonda V. Montgomery   60
David L. Morgan   60
Frank E. Moss   27
Daniel P. Moynihan   143
Robert J. Myers   61, 82
John F. Myles   61
Ralph Nader   123
Robert J. Newcomer   42,
   47, 54, 62
Howard N. Newman   63
Sandra J. Newman   63
M. Newton   43, 45, 64
Richard M. Nixon   6, 13
   14, 16, 96, 97, 98, 99,
   101, 102, 105, 106,
   108, 109, 110, 111
M.L. Noble   30
Barbara G. Odell   76
Tip O'Neill   124
Laura K. Olson   63
Jennifer O'Sullivan   63
Robert Packwood   128
T. Palcozolla   86
Howard A. Palley   63
Marian L. Palley   63
H.C. Palmer   75
L. Paringer   64
Beverly Patnaik   65
William A. Pearman   64
Carol C. Pegels   64

Claude Pepper   27, 28,
   131
R. Perot   108
Julian Pettengill   64
Penelope L. Pine   57,
   64
Nora Piore   65
Monte M. Poen   65
D.B. Potemken   59
Henry J. Pratt   65
Ronald Prihoda   40, 45,
   57
J. Thomas Puglisi   65
David L. Ransen   65
I. Raskin   79
Ronald Reagan   17, 18,
   20, 21, 27, 28, 130,
   131, 132, 133, 134,
   135, 136, 137, 138,
   139, 140, 143, 144,
   145, 146, 147
Frederic G. Reamer   65
Donald Regan   131
Uwe E. Reinhardt   65
Walter Reuther   90
Abraham Ribicoff   89,
   93, 95, 96, 113
Dorothy P. Rice   66
Bennett M. Rich   66
Elliott Richardson   100
H. Richmond   66
Christian Ritter   67
Alice Rivlin   112
Nelson A. Rockefeller
   92, 104
Franklin D. Roosevelt 6
Dan Rostenkowski   124
Julius A. Roth   67
Milford O. Rouse 90, 92
Julie Rovner   67
G. Rowe   42
Diane Rowland   38
Robert J. Rubin   67
Howard Rusk   83, 93
Martin Ruther   67

Subject Index

Self Concept of Elderly
Social Security   3, 4, 8,
   9, 10, 16, 17, 18, 25,
   30, 47, 59, 75
Social Security Act   43
Social Security Advisory
   Council   81, 86, 99, 114,
   115, 127, 130, 138, 139,
   140
Social Security Reform
   Commission   18
Social Security Trust
   Fund   8, 128, 143
Socialized Medicine
   British Model   9, 26,
   27, 50
Supplemental Insurance
   (Third Party)   3, 10,
   16, 19, 20, 35, 41,
   54, 55, 56, 66, 77
Stereotypes of Elderly
   (Ageism)   31, 46, 54,
   59

Tax Equity and Fiscal
   Responsibility Act
   18, 19
Title XVIII   3, 16
Title XX   33

Uniform Accounting/
   Reporting   16
Universal Needs Program
   5, 6, 23
U.S. Chamber of Commerce
   97
U.S. Congress
   Ways and Means Committee 8
U.S. Department of Health
   and Human Services
U.S. Department of Health,
   Education and Welfare
   10, 11, 15
U.S. Department of Justice
   11

U.S. General Account-
   ing Office   15
U.S. Government
   Documents
U.S. House of Repre-
   sentatives
   Select Committee on
   Aging   27
U.S. Office of
   Economic Opportunity
U.S. Senate
   Finance Committee
   10, 12
U.S. Supreme Court   11
Utilization Review
   16, 17

Voucher Payment Plan 30

White House Conference
   on Aging